Embracing Change

Embracing Change

Jana Firestone

Affirm press

Affirm press
books that leave an impression

Published by Affirm Press in 2022
28 Thistlethwaite Street, South Melbourne,
Boon Wurrung Country, VIC 3205
affirmpress.com.au
10 9 8 7 6 5 4 3 2 1

Title: Embracing Change / Jana Firestone, author.
ISBN: 9781922626776 (hardback)

NATIONAL LIBRARY OF AUSTRALIA
A catalogue record for this
book is available from the
National Library of Australia

Jacket design by Alissa Dinallo
Jacket author photograph by Chelsea Morley/Tiny Disco
Internal design by Emily Thiang
Printed and bound in China by C&C Offset Printing Co., Ltd.

This book is dedicated to every gentle soul who has been through the mire. We all have to find our own pathway out. If you're feeling the fear and are afraid to 'do it anyway', this book is for you. One step at a time, one foot in front of the other, you've got this.

To my boys (C, C & S) – thank you for allowing me to embrace my own change and supporting me all the way.

Contents

Introduction

As a therapist, people often ask me whether I too experience the issues that might be impacting the client in front of me. My answer is always a resounding YES! But knowing how to manage these issues and actually applying it to my own life is a whole other matter.

We know that the global pandemic has been a powerful catalyst for change, leading many of us to stop and reflect on the choices we have made in our lives. It's also given us a push towards thinking about what is important to us and what we would like to change in future to make us happier and more whole human beings. Some of us have made significant decisions about where we would like to be living, what kind of work we'd prefer to be doing, and the kinds of relationships we thrive in – or not. In some cases, these decisions come swiftly and with ease. But, for many of us, the concept of change can spark an avalanche of stress and anxiety, leaving us in a state of indecision.

We all approach life with our own unique set of experiences that inform our decisions and inhibit our choices. This doesn't mean they are set in stone and are impossible to shift – quite the opposite. Once we understand why we make the choices we do and what it is that's holding us back, the world is our oyster.

This book explores the psychological concepts that prevent us from taking the leap and embracing new ventures in our lives. It's presented in bite-sized, jargon-free chunks that will hopefully untangle the issues for you and leave you with concrete, tangible strategies you can start implementing immediately.

From Imposter Syndrome, Fear and Anxiety to Self-esteem and Grief, the aim of each chapter is to bring these concepts to life through sharing anecdotes from both the well-known guests who have appeared on my podcast, *The Curious Life*, and from my personal and professional life experience. I have faced many of these themes as challenges myself and share what's worked to help me move through some of the stickier parts of my own life.

The process of writing this book and unpacking the issues has been a whirlwind of adventure. Exploring these concepts in longform, as opposed to in session or in article or interview form, has given me the wonderful gift of insight in hindsight. Journeying through my own experiences of things like grief, anxiety or imposter syndrome has unfurled so many illuminating memories that have added to my own understanding. This exploration has also given me the opportunity to see my life in a different light and serves as a reminder that it's never too late to pause and reflect. While each of the themes relates to psychological theories and research, the key points are tied to real-life experiences and examples to provide practical advice from someone who has lived it and helped countless others survive it.

I hope that in sharing some of what I have learned through my own life stories and experiences here, you will also find moments of connection and realisation that help you move through whatever you might be feeling in this moment, and lead you to better roll with life's punches and embrace change. It is, after all, the only constant.

Grief

Grief is a universal, unavoidable, guaranteed life experience that each of us will encounter to varying degrees in our lifetime. For some, it stops us dead in our tracks, rendering us completely bereft, lost and stuck in our pain. For others, it can propel us forward and help us move through the stickiest parts to continue to achieve and evolve. Although grief can be a powerful mechanism for change, experiencing grief at a time when new opportunities might be on the horizon can make it difficult to identify those moments or recognise them as open doors.

For most of us, grief is forced upon us whether we like it or not. There is no rulebook as to why it can be a catalyst for change for some and yet make others fearful to approach anything new. The intensity of the grief and the resilience we may have to move through it can depend on many different factors, such as our age, our life experiences, the type of grief we are experiencing and what other stressors we are going through at the time.

The most important thing to note is that there is *no right or wrong way to grieve*. But it is imperative that we do the work in honouring the loss and identifying the impact on our lives from a present and future perspective, and we'll get into that a little bit further along.

My Own Journey

Grief is something I have intimate knowledge of, both personally and professionally, and with that came a deep understanding of how it can transform your life in powerful ways.

When I was 21 years old, my mother passed away suddenly and without warning. One minute she was there – always available at the end of the phone whenever I called (many, many times a day), the person who I shared every detail of my life with, who emanated love and unconditional support, and who shelled out the hard truths when they were required – then, overnight, she was gone.

The emptiness of losing someone you love remains with you for a long time. When we turned off the machines and walked away from the hospital for the last time, it felt like I had left a huge and vital fragment of myself in that room. Even now, 18 years later, that missing piece has never been filled in. There is no doubt that some of the best things that have happened in my life have occurred in the last 18 years, but nothing ever replaces that loss, that missing piece.

Unless you have experienced sudden and unexpected death, it's difficult to explain without sounding melodramatic. One day your whole world is complete; there is safety and security in everything that you do. The next moment, every part of your being is ricocheting with shock, disbelief, pain, desperation and a new understanding that nothing in this life is guaranteed. That in itself can be an incredibly jarring and alarming way to exist.

In my own experience, that moment of losing my mum, and the hollow disbelief and shock that followed, will stay with me forever. Our family of four, reduced to three, each of us aching in our distress and isolation, reeling with the loss and wondering how on earth we were going to accept this new existence. The emptiness in the house, in our hearts and by our sides stayed with us for the longest time.

When you lose someone you love, you feel maimed, shredded, like you're staggering around in a horror movie. Your entire world is shattered into a million irretrievable pieces, yet bizarrely the world keeps turning and the rest of the population goes about their business like they have no idea that the entire world is actually off its axis. Sometimes you want to scream at the innocent people on the street – 'DON'T YOU KNOW WHAT HAS HAPPENED?! HOW CAN YOU JUST BE WALKING AROUND LIKE NOTHING HAS HAPPENED?!' – and other times you just want to hide in your room and never come out again. Sometimes it's both at the same time.

You wake up every morning with the searing pain of the loss burning through you again and again in some cruel plot to make you suffer the loss anew each day. That's assuming you've actually been able to sleep the night before and, if you have, that you've made it through another night of relentless nightmares where you're desperately trying to change the outcome, saving her over and over again, finding the one thing that was missed so that she could make it through this time.

You reach for the phone every time something happens, with a crushing reality check a split second later when you realise what you're doing. You plaster on a smile and move through the crowds and become quite practised as a functioning ghost masquerading as a human, walking among the living.

No one ever forgets the moment when everything comes grinding to a halt. As a therapist, we are trained to disclose very little of our personal lives in session, except if it's going to be of therapeutic value to the client. For that reason, it is difficult for me to share my own personal story in such detail, but my hope is that, in doing so, it helps anyone who might be going through their own loss.

The first year of grief is a blur of intense and agonising pain. Sounds escape your body that you never thought possible. Strength appears in moments when you least expect it and you'll be surprised how resilient you actually are, even through the worst of it.

I often tease my father about the fact that he can't recall any of the things that happened in that first year. He'll laugh at me like I'm making it up when I recount something awful or funny or massive that happened. Grief does strange things to our minds when it's busy protecting us.

My parents had been together for thirty-five years when Mum died. They had the usual rollercoaster of highs and lows, but a deep connectedness and friendship that was evident to everyone around them. They were a team. I had just turned 21 and Mum lost consciousness on the eve of my brother's 18th birthday. Though I was dealing with my own loss, I was keenly aware of the losses my family and extended family were also going through. Grief looked very different for each of us. It affected us all in very different ways, and it still does today.

Grief will always be unique to the person experiencing it, no matter what threads tie you together. Though the experience itself is universal, the way through it can be as varied as the stars. The important thing to know is that you *will* find your way through it.

Grief evolves and changes over the years, but you never quite escape it. It's a shapeshifter lurking in the shadows, loud and present in some moments, and silently ebbing away, bleeding into your consciousness when you least expect it.

One of the early models of grief and one that is still talked about today is the Five Stages of Grief by Elisabeth Kübler-Ross.[1] The idea is that, as we grieve, we go through the five stages of denial, anger, bargaining, depression and acceptance. I certainly experienced most of those just in the hospital alone; however, there's a bit of a misconception around this theory. The five stages have been updated to seven in recent years, but, in my experience, these are certainly not concrete, nor do they occur in any set order. In fact, some people may not experience these stages at all.

The grieving process can be incredibly complex and different from one person to the next. It can be helpful to understand that grief will change over the years, but there is no set of instructions that will resolve it or expedite the process, unfortunately.

Grief can have such a profound impact on our lives, yet it can take on a remarkably different appearance, depending on where we are at in our lives and the type of loss that we experience.

In a relatively short period of time, I lost my maternal grandmother, my mother, my great aunt and my paternal grandmother. Just a few years before that, I also experienced the loss of my great uncle, another family member to suicide and a young friend to suicide also. Each of these losses was completely different and the way that I processed some of the earlier losses was vastly different to the way I processed the losses after my mum died. Sometimes, even now, if I hear of the death of someone I didn't even know, it can take me right into the depths of those grief feelings that I know so well. Other times, I'm much more able to hear the news and let it wash over me with more perspective.

Grieving Other Losses

Grieving a loss isn't always about a person dying. Not long after losing Mum and the entire top generation of my family, my relationship with my boyfriend at the time also came to an end. We had been living together for many years and had been close friends for a few years before that. It was my first significant, young-adult relationship and it took quite a long time for that to truly unravel.

The end of a relationship can mean the end of the hopes and dreams for a future you had once imagined. It can mean the loss of friendships and your place within a group. It can also take some time to rediscover who you are as an individual, when you are no longer part of a pair.

For me, it was all of those things. I noticed that I wouldn't be invited to 'couples dinners' with my closest friends and suddenly my value had changed. The change in my status also meant that I was then being viewed differently by a lot of people, both those close to me and complete strangers. As any woman who has been single as an adult can attest, being a single woman automatically characterises you as a predator in the eyes of many coupled-up women, simply by virtue of the fact that you're a single woman. It's a lot to process when you're coming to terms with being on your own again.

For me, losing a parent, my partner and my relatives all in a very short period of time really compounded the grief in many ways.

It took a toll emotionally and existentially. Perhaps the losses felt deeper and more difficult to move through because there were so many. Everything that identified me as the person I was in the world was ripped out from under me and I resented the fact that I had to be the one to put the pieces back together again. It took a long time for me to stop pretending I knew who I was and what I wanted in life, and to actually *know*.

Losing our identity as an individual is one of the many ways that grief can cause us to get stuck and find change difficult. It can take shape in many forms – the grief we experience after the end of a friendship, a business deal not going through, a job loss, parent separation, difficulty in personal relationships or any other situation where we feel we have lost something, where we feel we have not achieved something or as though something is missing. We can't always see a way out of these feelings, but, no matter how displacing that loss may be, there is always a way out. Sometimes it just takes perseverance, perspective and time.

The Closure Myth

We've all heard the saying 'time heals all wounds', but, unfortunately, it's not as straightforward as that. One of the big misconceptions about grief is the notion of closure. That, in time, you will experience closure and that's what to aim for. Closure implies that there is an end to the moment or the feeling you are trying to make sense of, that it will literally close the loop on the pain and the jagged loss, and, finally, that missing piece of the puzzle will come together to bring you peace.

I can tell you, both personally and professionally, closure does not exist. You never close the loop on the loss of someone you love. You just learn to live with it, one agonising day at a time.

In my time as a counsellor at the Coroners Court of Victoria, I worked with the families, friends and witnesses of sudden and unexpected deaths in Victoria. The majority of my clients were partners, parents, siblings or children of someone who had lost their life suddenly, without warning, through suicide, an accident or unthinkable tragedy.

Having my own experience with losing a parent suddenly, though not through the coronial system, allowed me to connect on a personal level with those incredibly brave people who were in the worst moments of their lives. In some cases, I sat with them in their grief for the entire time I was employed there, providing counselling and support throughout the lengthy coronial process. I helped interpret autopsy reports after meetings with forensic pathologists, facilitated the viewing of traumatic scene photos, advocated for families throughout the coronial investigation and supported many through lengthy and painful inquests.

Closure does not exist. You never close the loop on the loss of someone you love. But you can learn to live with it.

I also worked intensively with the families of the victims of the 2009 Black Saturday bushfires, who lost their loved ones in the most unimaginable circumstances. Their grief was palpable, irreparable, and rightfully so.

I often think of the families I worked with at the Coroners Court; their stories and their strength have stayed with me to this day. Although to some, working so closely with death sounds morbid and frightening, in fact it was one of the most rewarding jobs I have had. To be allowed to hold the space for someone emotionally, through their most private and unbearable pain, is an incredible honour and a privilege I didn't take lightly. The work was heavy and often very distressing, but, unlike in many other therapeutic roles, seeing the immediate impact of support made my own distress well worth it.

I frequently think of those courageous families who allowed me to be part of their story, and their resilience is something that I will hold close for the rest of my life. They showed me that, no matter how tragic the loss may be and how horrific the pain, there is always life beyond death. However, I don't think any of those families would say that they have ever felt closure in relation to the death of their loved one.

We need to change the language around loss, as it sets up unrealistic expectations that, when not achieved, can cause even greater harm to the person grieving. When there is a sense that we need to work towards a goal or a specific timeline that will mean an end to this intolerable pain, when we don't reach it, the feelings of loss, distress and hopelessness that are already such a huge part of grief can intensify and be compounded.

Embracing Change After Loss

For me, I was able to use the loss of my mother to move forward with my life. At the time, I had just turned 21 and was enjoying the freedoms that a young person playing grown-ups does. Life was all about my friends, going out at night (and staying up until sunrise) and working in a bar and as a part-time receptionist. I had studied musical theatre and was making the most of my 'figuring it out' year, shelving any ideas of a professional life for a later date and not being fussed by my lack of any clear direction.

Then, when my mum died, I applied for a psychology degree and commenced within nine months of her death. This wasn't necessarily a conscious choice. I didn't say to myself, 'now you need to make something of yourself'; it was more of a change in direction that occurred without my realising. Psychology was something I had always planned on pursuing at a later stage, but Mum's death propelled me forward, through the mud, through the darkness and into the next phase of my life. That certainly doesn't mean I stopped grieving or stopped feeling the pain and the loss; I just found myself growing up overnight and my priorities shifting.

This isn't the case for everyone. For many people, grief can leave you stuck in that mud, frozen in time at the point of the loss, unable to move forward. When that happens, change and progression can feel impossible.

The emotional ramifications of grief can go on for years. In fact, one of the themes that emerged in the conversations on my podcast, *The Curious Life*, was just how much it varies for each person, to come to a place of acceptance or, at least, to the realisation that the grief and loss aren't impacting daily life in an intrusive way anymore.

For some of my podcast guests it has been a longer road to the new normal and for others it has been less so. For *The Bachelor*'s Sam Wood, who lost his mother to cancer when he was a teenager, it took about ten years to get to a place where his mother's death wasn't consciously impacting him in a negative way anymore. He also explained that grief and recovery looked completely different for each of his younger siblings. The fact that grief can look so different within families is something that I have encountered a lot in my professional life and is often the source of much confusion and fraction between siblings. In Sam's case it illustrates the implications of age and roles within the family at the time of the loss. In some families, being the youngest who spent the least amount of time with a parent can mean less early grief but more complex grief later. For older siblings, who had the most time with a parent, the loss can be more acute, but the meaningful years together can also bring some comfort.

The pathway through grief within families is never uniform and we can't expect to move through it in a singular way. Understanding that each of us will walk our own path through the pain is an important realisation, alleviating us of comparison and judgement as we make our way through the mire.

Sam and I shared some moments of sadness together as we unpacked our respective losses, and I very much related to his experience of it taking about ten years to feel like the loss was not having daily implications. We also shared the ways we try to keep the memories of our mothers alive for our young children and how the loss can intensify once you become a parent yourself. This is one of the big issues I have with the notion of closure. When our lives inevitably continue without the person we love, it's important to know that these new life experiences and developmental stages might trigger our grief in a new and powerful way. This is not something to be afraid of, just a painful reminder again that grief is an ever-evolving, non-linear process that will take on different meaning at different times in our lives.

Sam is a terrific example of someone who has used a significant loss to inspire him to do great things. He told me that, in whatever he does, there's a part of him that's driven by the desire to make his mum proud. This is absolutely a theme in my own life and in some of the other moving conversations I have been lucky enough to take part in.

Bondi Sands founder Blair James went through many years and layers of grief and loss from the ages of 12 to 23, describing it as one hit after another. From a very comfortable family life and a move to the UK, to the family business losing money and eventually failing, resulting in the loss of the family home and significant financial hardship, to the sudden death of his father and then the death of his mother to cancer, Blair's story is tragic and devastating in every way. He has been through just about every kind of loss and grief experience there is and all at an incredibly young age. Blair described coming to terms with this in therapy only in the last few years, where he recognised for the first time the enormity of his losses and the cumulative grief he had been through.

Blair's story is incredibly powerful, not only because of the depths of his losses, but also because of how successful he has become despite them. He is a brilliant example of a person moving through their grief and not becoming stuck. He had the entrepreneurial spirit from an early age, but he would have been forgiven entirely if he had just crawled into a tight little ball and not left his room for a few years after the incredibly difficult hand he had been dealt. Despite the magnitude of his losses, Blair went on to build himself a little tanning business from the ground up with what little inheritance he had received and, in a relatively short period of time, turned that into a multimillion-dollar self-tanning empire that continues to grow and evolve today.

Do we need to be one of these special people to endure such losses and become great successes? Absolutely not. We can all use grief to transform our lives and make meaning out of the biggest life-altering losses. The challenge is, how do we find a way to shelve the pain and the anguish and push ourselves forward?

The key is to compartmentalise the grief. It is absolutely okay and, in fact, incredibly important to feel it and acknowledge that it's there, but then equally important not to let it dominate or interfere with your functioning. Don't get me wrong, there have been times when I haven't been able to sleep because of grief, times when I have been on the ground, howling and in utter, immovable distress. However, those are the moments – valuable, healing moments – that are the work of moving through grief. Feeling the pain, feeling the loss, then literally picking yourself up off the ground and putting one foot in front of the other to move forward.

In my case, it wasn't a matter of shelving and locking away the pain – the loss of my mother was very much present in everything I did in those early years and continues to be today. However, I have been able to use her death to motivate me to make decisions to better myself and progress my life. As a consequence, one of the greatest compliments I could ever receive will always be, 'Your mum would be so proud of you'.

This is something that resonated in my podcast conversation with Jules Sebastian, stylist, presenter, writer and wife of award-winning artist Guy Sebastian. During our interview and in her book *Tea & Honesty*, she shared the ways that she processed the inconceivable loss of her brother to suicide just five days after her wedding to Guy. Despite the enormity of the tragedy, early on, Jules accepted the fact that there would always be so many questions about his death that would forever be unanswered. She acknowledged that she would probably spend the rest of her life without the answers she yearned for. Coming to that place of acceptance is an incredibly therapeutic strategy.

We always want to resolve or make sense of the loss of someone we love, but, in so many cases, it's just not something that can ever be explained away. Coming to a resolution in your own mind, like Jules did, to accept that we may always have to live with the 'why' going unanswered, makes moving through the grief much more attainable. That doesn't mean the loss isn't still keenly felt, it just makes the one-foot-in-front-of-the-other part that little bit easier.

For Jules, she uses her brother's memory to motivate her and to do things that would make him proud. It would be entirely reasonable if Jules had also taken this blow and tucked herself away safely at home, unable to do anything for a long time. The fact that she has been able to take the pain and transform it into something positive, where some good can come out of something so tragic, means that she has been able to process the loss in a comprehensive way – acknowledging and accepting that questions will remain and counteracting the profoundness of the loss by giving her brother a meaningful, present and ongoing role in her life. When we do this, we are making sense of the senseless and giving ourselves parameters within which to function again.

I also spoke with seven-time world champion surfer Layne Beachley, who has been through immeasurable losses. Layne shared her story with me of losing three mothers – yes, three – and wading her way through a significant identity loss at a very young age. At the age of 6, her mother passed away suddenly and without warning. At the age of 8, her father revealed that she was adopted, and she had not been told of this before. This triggered a deep sense of abandonment and fear of rejection in Layne, but she described that revelation as the reason behind her drive and ambition to be the best. She decided, at that very young age, that if she wanted to be loved and accepted, she needed to become a world champion. And that she did, seven times over. For Layne, the grief continued into adulthood when she lost her biological mother and her stepmother to cancer. While many might spiral into darkness, Layne continues to use her difficult and devastating life experiences to inspire and motivate her in the choices that she makes for herself and shares her story and lessons learned with others.

Moving Through Grief

I want to be clear here again, though: you do not need to be a high-achieving major success, like my podcast guests are, to move through grief in a positive way. Every single one of us has the ability to process grief in the same way that my guests have. We are all capable of resilience when we have the right tools and support around us.

Death is an inevitable part of life. Loss is an inevitable part of life. Grief is an inevitable part of life. They all suck. But how we move through the worst of it and find the moments of lightness is how we pave the way for what's coming next.

It's important to talk through grief. Talk to the people you love, find others who have been through it too, and share your pain and feelings out loud. Taking the feelings from inside and getting them outside the confines of our own mind is incredibly important. This is how we process grief – how we make sense of it in our rational mind. It's how we acknowledge the loss and the repercussions to our being.

Writing can also be incredibly healing and helps us to decompress and move some of the weight from ourselves. I love a journal – a private space to write all the deepest, darkest parts of yourself out and leave them there in the pages of the book. Make a ritual out of it: spoil yourself with a beautiful journal, light a candle, put on some music and get it all out. Ambience may not be your thing, so, in that case, crack open a bottle of gin (or whatever your poison may be) and get rage-writing. It's absolutely okay to feel ripped off by the circumstances.

Write a letter to the person you have lost; write several. This can be a wonderfully healing exercise that keeps you feeling connected to your loved one. Don't be afraid to tell them how you really feel – how angry or how abandoned you feel, how broken or damaged their death made you feel. If it's the end of a friendship or relationship, all of that applies too.

Find a way to channel the energy of the waves of emotion into something that brings you relief, through exercise, creative outlets or something unique to you. Find ways to reconnect with people you love or, when you're ready, form new connections with people who get you.

Of course, I would always recommend finding a therapist that you connect with and using that space to work through the grief also. A professional is trained to hold the space for you, to provide you with a safe place to unload and unburden yourself, and to help you walk away a little bit lighter.

Admitting that you need help to deal with any kind of loss is showing your strength, not weakness. The more we hold things in and keep the pain to ourselves, the more complex and complicated it can become. To have the flexibility required to be able to embrace change, we need to water the gardens of our mind with tenderness and care.

Grief does so many things to change our perspective and, for many, marks the ending or beginning of a new chapter in our lives. These are the defining moments that index our periods of growth and change from which we can flourish. There will always be hangovers from our previous chapters that are the hallmarks of our grief, feelings like shame or guilt that can seep into our current chapters unannounced. We may be more sensitive to triggers or need to treat ourselves with more kindness at different points in the year. Anniversaries, birthdays, holidays and important dates will always be a time to be mindful of how we are managing in our new reality. Sometimes those dates can creep up on us and only make sense after we've had an overreaction to something innocuous. When that happens, we need to be kind to ourselves – not beat ourselves up.

Grief can make us feel wild and unhinged, untethered and lost. Remember that person who felt all of those things when you have some distance from the event. That person who will still be inside, buried deep within, who needs love and understanding when they leap out from the shadows to respond to a trigger. That person, who might fly off the handle or hurt someone they love because of the pain they are feeling, needs compassion and soothing before being gently returned to their resting place. That part of us remains to protect us, to remind us that we have been through the worst, most unbearable pain and that life will never be the same again. Not that we consciously need reminding of that, but that's how our minds work – leaving a part of us behind to shield us from the worst and safeguard our hearts. Acknowledging *that* part of ourselves, accepting that it exists and resisting the urge to extinguish its flame, is one of the ways we begin to heal. In other words, don't fight it – listen to it. If that part of you fires up, ask yourself why. What does that little part of you need? Maybe it's a big old cry or a large glass of something (not every time!), but taking a moment to honour the feelings that have been activated is all part of the work.

Change doesn't have to be as scary as grief can be. Knowing that we can move through the hardest, most unbearable days of our lives is the little kernel of hope to keep in your back pocket, so that if and when you find yourself in this position, be assured that there will be a way out.

Hack

Grief is evolving and so are you.

Check in

What do I need to listen to right now?

How can I honour those feelings?

Self-talk

My feelings are valid and it's okay to feel them.

The Work

Feel all the feelings, don't push them away. Find a method that works for you, to express the loss and move through the layers in a way that's meaningful to you. Try writing, journalling, gratitude journals, letters to loved ones, talking with family, friends or a professional and allowing yourself to break open the wound without fear. Understand that there may be no closure, but an evolution of your understanding of the loss. Find ways to honour your loved one and keep them alive in your thoughts, and share them with the people you love. Above all else, remember to be kind to yourself, especially if it's taking a little longer to find your new normal.

Imposter Syndrome

Behind many successful and not-so-successful people is a nagging, critical inner voice telling us we are just not good enough. That destructive little naysayer is often the loudest and most convincing voice, talking us out of moving forward, taking the leap and believing in ourselves. This bad boy has a name and has aptly been identified as imposter syndrome.

Most people will go a few rounds with this guy at some point in their lifetime. In fact, a quick internet search will bring up endless lists of highly successful people who have talked about their relationship with imposter syndrome. People like Tina Fey, Lupita Nyong'o, Meryl Streep, Lady Gaga – the best of the best. Resoundingly, their thoughts and feelings about themselves oscillate between complete belief in their skills and talents and a fear of being found out as a fraud.

You don't need to be signing multimillion-dollar entertainment deals to know what that feels like. In fact, this book itself may not have been written had I listened to my own noisy imposter syndrome. When the call came from the wonderful publishers at Affirm Press, I found myself in a meeting with the directors who had discovered my work and were inviting me to have a go at flexing my writing muscles with them. For anyone who is a fan of the television series *Younger,* you can imagine what it must have been like. I had gone from a therapist and podcaster to suddenly living out a scene from the hit show, being wooed by a publishing company and asked to share my thoughts with the world.

For me, the meeting was peppered with moments of reality, feeling daunted and overwhelmed, and that nagging sensation that, at any minute, someone was going to tap me on the shoulder and tell me I was at the wrong table, in the wrong meeting, that the publishers had mixed me up with someone else.

Even as I went home to think about their offer and hash out a few concepts, I managed to convince myself that I couldn't possibly write anything, that I had nothing to say and that even if I did, it wouldn't be useful to anyone. Imposter syndrome at its finest.

Through conversations with my friends and family and the stabilising force that is my incredible manager, I tried to tune out that spiteful noise and focus on the task at hand. As soon as I shelved the negativity (in reality, let it sit quietly at the back of the room and not pay it any attention), it gave me the space to start creating. The energy that I would have put into discrediting my abilities and swatting away the confidence being generously shared by the people around me was put to good use and redirected into the project.

That certainly doesn't mean I have conquered the self-doubt, not by a long shot. But I have been able to acknowledge it and resist the temptation to be pulled into the vortex by it. I made a conscious decision not to overthink it, not to get in my own way and just to embrace the incredible opportunity in front of me.

Who, Me?

For some people, their encounters with imposter syndrome may be fleeting, or occur at a volume that can be drowned out by the positive interactions and achievements or accolades that come their way. For others, the interaction can be far more lasting and damaging.

How is it that this negative, disparaging commentary can have so much power and earn the most points in the mental votes we tally in our heads?

Let's start at the beginning. The term 'imposter syndrome' was coined by psychologists Pauline Rose Clance and Suzanne Imes[2] in 1978. During their research, they discovered that a significant number of highly successful women felt they had fraudulently entered their professions and positions of power, despite earning those achievements through their own merits.

For so many people, and particularly women, this is the background noise in their own successes and failures. It's that inner critic saying, 'you're not good enough', 'you're not smart enough', 'you're a fake'. This theme is also the common thread in the stories that celebrities have shared publicly of their own experiences with imposter syndrome, no matter how successful they are. All too often they would circle back to the sense or the fear that they will be found out as untalented or unworthy and ousted from their careers. The fear that the truth will come out and the whole world will know that, actually, they can't act or sing or run a successful business.

At the time of Clance and Imes's research, they found this phenomenon to be much more prevalent in successful women, but it is now far more common to hear about the experience appearing in a much wider range of people, including men. Another swift internet search will tell you that Tom Hanks, Neil Armstrong and Robert Pattinson are among some of the highly successful men at the top of their game who have described feeling the same doubt about their careers and abilities, despite their success.

Weapons Down

In my conversation with Australian jewellery designer, entrepreneur and writer Samantha Wills for *The Curious Life* podcast, she shared her own deeply rooted experience with imposter syndrome. In fact, it has been such a prevalent force in her life that it was just about given the honour of a third-person resurrection in a character of its own throughout her debut book, *Of Gold and Dust*. In it, Samantha wrote in detail about the influence that imposter syndrome has had over her ability to take risks and trust her talents over the years.

As a wildly successful creative and businesswoman, on the surface Samantha appears to have had it all. Having built a glamorous empire and a life that saw her travelling the world, living in New York and at the helm of a thriving business, it would be safe to assume that she pretty well had things under control. However, what she found was the brighter her career burned, the louder her imposter syndrome became.

Eventually, and after decades on the battlefield, Samantha made a conscious choice to stop fighting that voice. Exhausted from trying to overcome the issue, she discovered that there is no easy way to turn that channel off. Instead, she chose to turn the volume down. In doing so, she found that her best weapon was to learn to live alongside it.

Now, instead of becoming stuck in procrastination, Samantha has chosen to take the power out of that painfully sharp inner critic by unravelling its secret. The secret being, in Samantha's words, that all imposter syndrome really is is an excellent fictional storyteller. By allowing ourselves to listen to the false narrative created by this wicked storyteller, we begin to believe it – line by line, chapter by chapter.

For many, it's this false narrative that makes it impossible to take the leap and become immersed in a new venture. We know that change can be scary enough, but it can become even scarier when we allow the seeds of self-doubt to bloom into forests of insecurity.

While many of my guests on the podcast have talked about their experiences with imposter syndrome and self-doubt, another that stands out is New Zealand–born (and Australianclaimed) actor Michala Banas. Michala has been working in film and television since she started out in advertising at 18 months of age. She has worked in some of the most successful television franchises and with some of the most powerful and impressive giants of the entertainment industry worldwide. Our conversation took an interesting turn when we started to talk about the phenomenon of imposter syndrome. Michala shared that even after 35 years in the industry, as a working actor and filmmaker, she still has moments where she questions her capabilities and whether she has what it takes for longevity in the business.

Instead of letting that dominate her thinking and slow her down, Michala has continued to forge ahead in her creative career, exploring new projects and training as an intimacy coordinator. Interestingly though, she readily admitted that she would love to create her own piece of work and stretch herself in ways she hasn't felt ready to do yet. So, it's a bit of a mixed bag – feeling confident to explore new skills but perhaps not quite believing in herself enough to leap off and into the deep end. For Michala, having those whispers of imposter syndrome is something she acknowledges but doesn't allow to control her story.

The aim for all of us is not to obliterate that inner critic and send it to live on another planet, although that would be nice. We just need to find a way to coexist, without giving it permission to take control and prevent us from trying new things. Acknowledge that it's there, give it a little pat on the head and then march right past.

Imposter Syndrome in Relationships

One of the other ways that imposter syndrome can show up uninvited is in the way we feel and behave in relationships. If we are living with an internal dialogue of self-doubt that questions our deservedness, it can create insecurity and a sense of not being enough for our partner. When this occurs, it can lead to unhealthy relationships that can sometimes look like neediness, overcompensating, compliance or even self-sabotage.

Reflecting on the relationships that didn't work out in my own past, particularly as a young person without the depth of experience and maturity I have all these years later, there were many instances where I accepted behaviours and allowed the expectations of my partners to be the priority.

In early relationships, I often allowed my partners to direct the rules of engagement. As a result of one particular relationship, I developed a crippling toilet phobia in the following relationships. I would go to extreme lengths to mask the uncontrollable sound that inevitably occurs when we need to go. And I'm talking about number ones! That relationship had instilled the semiconscious belief in me that women didn't do gross things like go to the bathroom. And that if they did, we wouldn't be good enough or attractive enough in our relationships. I carried that paranoia with me for many, many

Acknowledge your inner critic, give it a pat on the head and then march right on past.

years after that relationship. It took the total disbelief and dismantling of that fear of rejection by my current partner to rebuild the confidence I had in myself as a worthy partner.

Toilet phobia aside, I have always considered myself to be a strong (and strong-willed), independent woman who would never allow a man to dictate what happens in my life. However, with self-doubt comes an astonishing power to eat away at the strongest of standards.

Of course, like many things, we often don't notice these patterns of behaviour or the quietly eroded standards until we have the benefit of hindsight – or in this case, a healthy relationship against which to measure the not-so-great ones.

What Can We Do About It?

Perhaps, like Samantha Wills or Michala Banas, we can earn to live alongside our imposter syndrome with a no-nonsense approach. When that negative inner critic creeps in, take a leaf out of Samantha's book and negotiate with it. 'Okay, I know you're there and you're clearly not going away, but give me 10 minutes to do this task', and immerse yourself in the doing, rather than in the second-guessing. Often when we throw ourselves into the thing that we are avoiding, we can distract ourselves just enough to actually get going.

If you find your self-doubt intensifying, ask yourself for the evidence. Is the belief founded? Or is it a grand scheme concocted by your self-doubt, that mischievous storyteller on a mission to sabotage any plans you might have had for taking the leap?

Collect evidence to support the belief that you *are* good enough. Make a list of the people who believe in you, who have hired you, who listen to you. Make another list of all the things you are brilliant at, the things you have achieved, the milestones you have reached in your personal and professional life. That is the evidence that the imposter syndrome is trying to negate.

In relationships, try to evaluate whether you have established patterns of behaviour over time that mean that your needs aren't being met. How do you react during arguments? Can you gauge whether you are sabotaging the relationship in any way? If the answer is yes, circle back to your self-talk. Pull out the journal and pen and write down all the things you believe about yourself and what you deserve from your relationship. Once you have identified which parts of your inner dialogue belong to imposter syndrome, collect the evidence that supports the opposite. Then fire that fraud-mongering cynic that is monologuing in the background and send it away to the furthest corner of your mind.

As a therapist, I frequently talk my clients through this minefield, but I do understand, walking the walk can be a whole other beast!

Hack

Imposter syndrome is self-doubt creeping in.
Don't let it in and don't give it the power.

Check in

Which voice is louder? The inner critic or the one cheering me on?

Self-talk

It's okay for me to feel nervous about a new venture, but I'm just going to give it my best shot.

The Work

Acknowledge that needling, negative voice when it weasels its way in, but practise putting it to one side. Remember that, when it creeps in, it's just your mind's way of telling you that you feel uncomfortable or out of control. Use strong affirmations and positive self-talk to remind yourself that, although you may be feeling out of your depth or unsure of the next steps, you are going to try anyway. Remind yourself of the positives and your strengths and combat the self-doubt by bringing the evidence to the fore. Stockpile the evidence and keep it handy to bring out every time that voice tries to creep back in to negate the attempts at discrediting. You can do this!

Anxiety

Anxiety, my old friend. My nemesis. The silent partner in most of my transactions. The villain I'm running from in the movie of my life, on most days – good or bad. Funnily enough, it's also the same villain that appears to be chasing down most of the clients I've seen over the last decade and a half, not to mention my friends and family who have shared their own versions of the same gremlin invading their spaces when they least expect it.

Anxiety can be a huge roadblock to change, if we allow it to be. It can feed self-doubt and insecurity and prevent us from taking the risks that might be exactly what we need at the time. It can keep us feeling stuck and in a perpetual cycle of fear.

Anxiety is a natural part of the human experience, showing up whenever we might be facing something new. While some level of anxiety is expected and, in fact, can be helpful at times, when it becomes bigger than we can manage, it can mean decision-making and leap-taking become almost impossible.

You might have heard of the fight, flight or freeze response. It's our body's natural response to stress or danger, causing our nervous system to propel us into action or defence mode. Our ancestors needed those responses to survive, alerting them to very real threats to existence. Anxiety can trigger those responses in us too. In the modern era, those responses can be triggered by stress or an unconscious perceived danger that might seem trivial by the life-or-death triggers of our caveman ancestors' standards. However, if the perceived threat is giving up the security of your current role and taking a risk by starting anew elsewhere, that could very much trigger a freeze response that might mean avoiding the risk altogether. This is one of the ways we can get stuck and deny ourselves the opportunity to make changes that might actually be good for us.

The first step in breaking free of the chains of anxiety is understanding how it's happening and why.

How Anxiety Works

Most people experience anxiety in some form throughout their lives. You might be reading this thinking, 'nah, not me'. Well, read on and you might be surprised about the ways that anxiety probably *is* part of your life, perhaps in a positive way.

Talking about anxiety and living with anxiety has become much more normalised in recent years and thankfully it is now widely acknowledged and discussed. The more we share our experiences, the easier they become to manage.

For some people, living with anxiety can be entirely crippling and can mean the difference between getting out of bed that day or hiding under the covers for the next twenty-four hours. It might mean that phone calls and text messages go unanswered and social interactions are avoided.

Anxiety is a
natural part of the
human experience,
showing up whenever
we might be facing
something new.

It can look like overthinking, excessive worry and analysis of every thought and interaction. Sometimes it presents as high stress, reactive responses or feeling overwhelmed. It can also take the form of aggression – snapping at people or loved ones when feeling out of control.

Physically it might feel like spurts of a quickened heartbeat, numbness or difficulty breathing. This can trigger irrational thoughts that you're dying or about to die or that someone you love will die, with no evidence to support that at all.

The presentation of anxiety is as varied as we are and may look different on different days. On some days it can feel like a minor little niggle in the back of your mind, alerting you that something is not right. On others it can feel like a slow eruption of fear that blindsides you and takes you out of your own body until you're able to be tethered back down to earth again.

Most commonly, the anxious thoughts and the overthinking that can sometimes trigger an episode tend to invade in the quietest part of the day – right as we're about to go to sleep. It's a cruel ploy that lures us into a false sense of security, thinking we're tired and ready for sleep, and then *boom*! The minute we're alone in the quiet of the night, surrendering to our many thoughts and without the distractions of the day bubbling along around us, anxiety flexes its increasingly mighty muscles and takes hold.

For some, that can result in hours awake, worrying about the many things that we shouldn't be worrying about and stressing about the fact that we're not sleeping when we need to be. Or it might mean frequent sleep interruptions throughout the night or that we wake in the early hours and can't go back to sleep.

This vicious cycle can be utterly exhausting. When we're feeling anxious, we are flooding our systems with cortisol (the stress hormone) and adrenaline (the go-go-go hormone). Feeling anxious, fighting anxiety or recovering from an episode all take a huge amount of energy as our systems try to recalibrate, which is why, for so many people, anxiety can be debilitating. It can lead to procrastination, low mood, irritability and avoidance. Naturally, we tend to avoid and resist the things that make us feel anxious, which is why it can be one of the biggest barriers to change.

The Anxiety Shadow

I have always had a low level of anxiety operating in the background. Even as a young child I have distinct memories of that nauseous feeling creeping up over me as we drove to school pretty much every day of one particular year, for what seemed like no apparent reason. I was a happy child with lots of friends and, up until that point, things had been quite easy for me.

That year in primary school, however, I had a teacher who made me feel incredibly anxious about going to school. Prior to that year I had loved going to school. My teachers had always been incredibly kind and nurturing and made the classroom a safe space to be in. With this particular teacher, I was always afraid to be called on in class and literally felt sick to my stomach at the thought of not having my times tables memorised beyond the fives. I had witnessed occasions where she had lost her temper and told other students off in an angry tone. There was an edge to her that was very different to the nurturing I'd experienced with previous teachers. To my 8-year-old mind, this was incredibly frightening.

What would the teacher think of me? Would she yell at me? Tell me off in front of the other kids? Would they think I was stupid? Or a loser? Would I be the only one who didn't know the answer? I may not have articulated those exact thoughts so clearly in my mind at the time, but they were definitely the big feelings I was battling around the age of 8. So much so, that I actually convinced myself that I was unwell. So unwell, in fact, that I needed to stay home, wrapped up in bed for several weeks.

It's obvious to me now that it was anxiety, but at the time I had convinced my young self that I truly wasn't feeling well and needed to stay home. I convinced my doctor that I was unwell and even my parents, who were the biggest sceptics of them all when it came to us kids trying to pull the wool over their eyes, bought it for the most part.

I remember days spent lying in my parents' bed 'resting' and trying to recite and cement my times tables, to make the most of the time away from school, in an attempt to get ahead. This inability to rest and let go of the things I *should* be doing is a boundary I still have trouble with today, even when I genuinely am sick. But we are all a work in progress, right?

Memorising my times tables comfortably up to elevens gave me some relief when I finally returned to school. However, that sense of dread and fear and an internalised need to turn and run as I approached the school stayed with me for quite some time after. That little flurry of butterflies swirling in my stomach urging me to escape would appear out of nowhere throughout the day and I would have to fight the desire to leave the room while also battling the fear of being called on by the teacher. That's quite a combination for a little person to deal with each day. Some days, of course, were better than others and being called on when I knew the answer was a terrific antidote. But because I had no choice, I just had to ride it out and get through the year. The little vestiges from that time, however, left invisible scars in my psyche that changed the way I viewed the world and made the landscape a little bit scarier.

Anxiety continues to be an ever-present shadow in my life today, though it takes on quite a different shape now. I can be aware of it in the background on occasion, just a little ignorable niggle, or it can come charging in, bowling me over with physical sensations that are too troubling to ignore,

Anxiety is our
body's natural
response to
stress or danger.

sending me spiralling into a fear of dying. For me, that can be a twinge in the left arm (heart attack), twinges in the head (brain aneurysm), heart palpitations (any kind of coronary incident) or a general light-headedness that makes me feel like I'm losing my grip.

The most frightening experience I have had of this out-of-body anxiety occurred while I was driving on a freeway, with my children strapped into their car seats, asleep in the back. We were heading off on a camping holiday with friends and as we approached the Westgate Bridge, I began to feel the anxiety curling upwards inside my stomach, heart racing, my jaw clenching and internal alert systems pinging in my brain. I told my partner I was starting to feel anxious, and he tried to talk to me calmly and help me come down from that terrifyingly heightened state of physiological arousal.

The panic escalated with the realisation that there was no safe way for me to stop the car and switch places with him, with the threatening enormity of the freight trucks hurtling past us at speed exacerbating my fear to its peak.

With no other alternative, and feeling as though I was about to lose control of my arms and legs and then the steering wheel, I jerked the car into the emergency lane just at the point where the six lanes of traffic converged, before heading for the bridge.

It was an incredibly risky manoeuvre and one that didn't offer any real solution.

After taking a few moments to try to calm down, doing some controlled breathing and willing my shaking hands to be still, I realised that to get us out of this precarious situation, I would have to drive the car over the bridge and pull over when there was a safe place to do so.

My recollection of the event is much more composed than the incident itself, where I was in a frenzied state, forced into a state of quasi-control so that I could get my family off the verge of the busy freeway and over the bridge to safety.

Once I felt ready, I pulled the car back out of the emergency lane and moved towards the entrance to the bridge. Any shred of control or calm I had mustered in those last moments vanished the minute I accelerated. Again, I felt light-headed and as though my limbs were detached from my body. I slowed the car down to about 40 km/h – a dangerous move in itself, given the speed limit and velocity of the vehicles hurtling past me. I crawled across the bridge, heart racing, whimpering and on the edge of hysteria, feeling totally out of control of my body and as though, at any moment, the car would take flight over the side of the bridge or be the cause of a significant accident involving any of the cars or trucks that passed me.

Hands shaking, we made it over the bridge and into a petrol station, where I spent some time recovering from the intensity of the experience. Amazingly, my children slept through the entire ordeal and woke up none the wiser!

As for me, this was a real turning point in my anxiety. I had never experienced anything quite as severe as this incident and was taken by surprise at the power that it had over me. Having worked with clients for many years who suffer from panic attacks and knowing their second-hand accounts in intimate detail still did not prepare me for my own experience.

Anxiety does not discriminate. You can know everything there is to know about the presentation and treatment of anxiety, but applying it to yourself in real time, during a real event, isn't necessarily so easy.

After that experience and for a long time afterwards, any high speed (greater than 60 km/h) or open-road driving would elicit an immediate anxiety response in me. My cortisol and adrenaline would start pumping, my heart would race and repetitive, intrusive thoughts would intervene, convincing me that I would be run off the road in some way.

Cognitively, I knew that these kinds of episodes would occur more frequently when I was tired, stressed or feeling overwhelmed in the various facets of my life. Sometimes just knowing that I would have to enter part of the local highway for a few kilometres to get to where I was going would be enough to trigger the physiological response.

One of the strategies I used to combat that was focusing on my breathing. When our nervous system is activated by anxiety, our breathing becomes shallow, which tricks our mind into thinking something is wrong. When I can slow my breathing down, with intentional, low, deep belly breathing, I can slow down my heart rate and buy myself some time to pull over if need be or to calm my nervous system down to a manageable level. While I'm doing that, I use positive self-talk to essentially talk myself down from the ledge. I remind myself calmly that I'm experiencing anxiety, that I'm perfectly safe and in control of the car. On repeat.

If we can address the physiological symptoms, we can trick our minds into a feeling of safety.

Know Your Boundaries

For one of the guests on my podcast, anxiety was the unexpected topic of discussion from the moment we sat down to chat. Sarah Davidson, who you might know as *Spoonful of Sarah* or from her podcast *Seize the Yay*, would certainly consider herself a Type A personality with a very busy life and high motivation and drive. Going hand in hand with those traits, as it so often does, is the unfortunate side-effect of anxiety.

The first thing Sarah shared with me was just how close she had come to cancelling the interview that day, after having been in the throes of intense anxiety that morning. Unfortunately, this was not a new or unusual experience for her. Through the first moments of our chat, she described how, just about every four to six weeks, she finds herself curled up in the foetal position, crippled with worry that completely impedes her ability to do anything at all. This is her own internal alert system warning her to immediately stop the myriad things that she is doing, to listen to her body and reset.

Sarah shared the frustration she feels with herself when it creeps up on her, despite knowing all too well what the many ingredients are that lead her into these episodes. Like so many of us that suffer from anxiety, somehow each month rolls around and Sarah finds herself ignoring all of those warning signs and paying the price again. And then again. And again.

While we might know that a lack of exercise, sleep, down time and self-care can trigger an episode or that being on that perpetual hamster wheel of busyness and overwhelm can lead to one, knowing and acting on it are two different things. Sure, we might know that we need to do A to avoid B, but when we're in the middle of the whirlwind of life and family, career and aspirations, actually taking the time to listen to the mind and body can be a whole other challenge.

For Sarah, the biggest challenge she faced as she began her career both as a legal professional and as a self-styled 'funtrepreneur' was learning to pace herself. Initially she found herself saying yes to everything, with very few boundaries and ignoring all the signs of fatigue and burnout. Two bouts of adrenal fatigue later, she realised that it just wasn't sustainable and that she would have to learn to say no. This was particularly complicated as Sarah battled her innate sense of gratitude for all the wonderful opportunities that were coming her way. Learning to say no and establishing firm boundaries can feel like one of the most difficult things to do, especially for someone with a Type A personality, high drive and motivation, and a career on the rise.

Sarah's story is a healthy reminder that we all need to keep a close eye on our boundaries. Once we start saying yes to things when we really mean maybe or no, it's a slippery slope to burnout and overload. Our boundaries are what help us to guard our most precious resources and protect us from energy and mental depletion.

This kind of burnout doesn't just happen to the highly successful Sarah Davidsons of the world; it can happen to anyone. For so many of us, including Sarah, we are that little duck sitting on the top of the water, appearing to have it all together, calmly floating through life without a single ruffled feather in sight. Yet as we all know, underneath the surface those little webbed feet can be madly thrashing about, just trying to keep us afloat.

Establishing clear and firm boundaries and learning to say no to the things we just don't have the space for is a huge part of managing our mental health and keeping anxiety at bay.

To do this, first you need to acknowledge that the purpose of these boundaries is to preserve your energy and mental health and ensure there is enough to pour into the things you love. Make a list of priorities, the parts of your life that *need* a yes, be that in time or energy, and let those be where you draw the line. Anything beyond that on a certain day or week has to wait.

It's also important to listen to your gut instinct. If the offer, proposal or request doesn't give you a resounding yes response in your gut, then it has to be a no. As tough as it can be to feel like you're letting someone down or that you *should* be feeling yes in response to a request to catch up with someone you love or to do something exciting, if your immediate reaction is a bit of a squirm, it has to be a no. Use that time to practise active self-care and infuse some rest and recovery into your schedule. Doing this will help untangle some of the chaos that creeps into our minds when we're busy and clear some space for the right opportunities to arise.

Health Anxiety

For many of us who suffer from anxiety, the tendency to jump to conclusions when we notice any sensation within our bodies is a common experience. Just a quick glance back over my own story will tell you I'm no stranger to it myself. The focused concern that we may be developing an illness or suffering from a health condition can range from fleeting or repeated thoughts all the way to a significant preoccupation that can become debilitating.

It's important to acknowledge the impact of the global pandemic on the psyche of the world, particularly for those of us with a tendency towards overthinking or worry. For many people, the constant barrage of alarming information about the pandemic, the rolling case numbers and death tolls, as well as repeated and lengthy lockdowns, have triggered a hypervigilance around health and wellbeing in ways that may not have been experienced before. For others, the pandemic may have prompted an awareness about mortality for the first time and that in itself can be a frightening experience.

As a global community, we have been subjected to a prolonged collective consciousness of the world being a scary place, making us fearful of others, eroding the safety of our local communities and narrowing access to our lives as we knew them. There is no doubt that the change in perspective has brought about a dynamic shift in priorities.

If the pandemic has heightened your anxiety around your own health and safety, there are ways to reduce this. When you notice you're having excessive negative thoughts about a sensation in your body, challenge that thought with a reality test. If you're experiencing a headache, for example, and start to panic that it's something more significant, make a list of all the possible reasons you might be experiencing that headache.

Could you be dehydrated, tired, stressed, carrying tension? Are you hungry or have you spent a long time at the computer? If you are able to distract yourself from the sensation, that's usually a pretty good sign that it's a symptom of anxiety or at least a non-life-threatening condition and you can reassure yourself that way. Build up an artillery of evidence to use against the worries as they arise, refocusing your energy into something that will help you to feel better.

Distraction and exercise are a brilliant way to tackle both health anxiety and more generalised anxiety, and keeping track of how often it occurs is particularly important. If you're noticing a pattern with your thinking or in relation to specific times or events, that will also form part of the evidence for your reality check – that you know you feel this way when … Gaining control of our thinking is all about positive self-talk, concrete evidence and a reframe:

- I notice I feel this way when …
- I'm not actually unwell, I'm just feeling worried about the current situation.
- I am healthy and strong and my body is doing its job to keep me well.

It goes without saying that, if you have genuine concerns about your health, it is always good to talk with your doctor.

Anxiety for Good

Although we mostly hear about the negative impacts of anxiety, from a psychological perspective it is actually considered to be one of the great motivators. It gives us that edge with a burst of adrenalin to take the leap and get outside of our comfort zone. It reminds us that the things we do or want are important to us, by giving us that little zing and flutter of tummy butterflies that help us to perform. It warns us when something might not be right or when we might be unsafe. It's an incredibly complex and brilliant little system that acts as though it operates outside our control, while sitting deep within our subconscious.

Think about a time when you might have had to do some public speaking or a presentation at work – it's likely that a healthy dose of anxiety helped get the best performance out of you. How did you feel at the time? Were you concerned about how you might be perceived? Worried that you might stumble over your words or not get your message across clearly? We all need that little nudge of anxiety, ensuring us to do our best.

On the flipside of that, maybe you recall a time when you didn't feel any of those nerves before talking in front of a group of people and perhaps it didn't go as well as you would have liked. The absence of healthy anxiety can sometimes lead to a flat performance or a lack of dynamism that takes you to the next level.

In a social setting, a little of that healthy energy is also a good thing. Are there ever times when you're supposed to be going to a party or out on a date and your anxiety is trying to convince you to stay home wrapped up in your dressing-gown? Do a little check-in. When you first accepted the invitation, were you excited by the prospect? If so, when did that anticipation become uncomfortable? Listen to your gut. If your initial response was positive, perhaps it's just anxiety creeping in and coaxing you back to the couch. Those moments when we push through that anxiety and move through the discomfort are often when we surprise ourselves by actually having a good time! Some of the credit for that get-up-and-go may be due to that little internal propellor pushing you out the door and giving you a little boost of energy to be the best version of yourself.

There are lots of ways that a little kick of anxiety can be a good thing and we may not even be aware that it's happening. It pushes us out of our comfort zone so we can rise up to the challenge. Without that little zing, we might not take those risks that can end up bringing the greatest reward.

Knowing that a little anxiety is a good thing can be difficult to rationalise when it starts creeping up or begins to feel out of control. In fact, knowing that it is beginning to spiral out of control can be the worst feeling in the world – a combination of fear and panic and that terrifying fusion of both real and imagined physical and psychological symptoms. Our nervous system can be pretty convincing and, once it fires up, the message we receive is that we are not okay.

The key to a happier existence is learning how to tame your anxiety and corral it into a force for good. When that familiar feeling starts snaking its way through your body, alerting you to the perceived danger ahead, consider how to take the power away from its stealthy attempts at a system overthrow. Use self-talk to remind yourself that you're feeling a bit nervous because you care about the task at hand and you want to do your best, that it's energy asking to be redirected to bring out the best in you.

So how do we tame the beast? The key to understanding anxiety is knowing that it feeds off control. The more attention we give it, the more powerful it becomes. That in turn becomes a vicious cycle that can be challenging to break.

One of the frustrating things about anxiety is that we may know exactly what exacerbates it, what is causing it, what is driving it, but still feel completely powerless to stop it. When the pressure feels like it's tightening around our chest, what can we do to release it?

The first step is loosening the grip of power that anxiety has over us. Every clinician talks about acknowledging anxiety. Giving it a name or an identity outside of yourself. That might sound a little bit strange at first, but, if we can find a way to recognise what is anxiety while we're in the midst of it, the vice grip releases bit by bit. Taking the driving anxiety as an example, if you find that you're feeling a physical symptom in the car – be it shallow breathing, light-headedness, perhaps a twinge in the left arm that sends you into panic mode – start by telling yourself you are okay and that it's just anxiety. Remind yourself that you are safe in your body and you are safe in the car.

Practise and repeat.

Telling ourselves we are okay and believing it can take a little time to sink in and become the louder voice we hear in our head. For some people, finding positive affirmations that resonate can be helpful to repeat or coming up with a line or two that you can calmly recite to yourself can bring you back into the moment and out of your head.

Another useful tool for getting out of your head and into your body is to use grounding techniques that can be done anywhere. There are countless suggestions online, and it's a good idea to try out a few to work out what suits you best. One I like to use is the 3-3-3 rule – name three things you can see, three things you can hear and move three parts of your body. Do this while you try to regain control of your breath by taking slow breaths in through the nose and holding, then out through the mouth to a count of three. This is a great little strategy to use in other situations too, when you might need a moment to breathe and calm yourself. (Any parents of preschoolers here? Remind me to take my own advice on that one, please!)

For those of us that might be stuck in the vortex of *doing*, it might help to know that there is a link between highly motivated people and anxiety, just as there is with perfectionism and anxiety. Sometimes having either (or both) of those traits can mean that just the mere idea of stepping off the treadmill can lead to anxiety. But, just like everything else in life, moderation is the key. If a schedule is what keeps your anxiety at bay, then try scheduling in the down time and self-care activities you know you need to keep the machine running.

In fact, putting together a work/play schedule that is realistic and achievable will go a long way in calming the mind and slowing down the nervous system. If we know a rest is coming up and that we aren't going to lose any valuable work time, that can be a panacea in itself.

If we can gain control of our thoughts around anxiety, get practised at using our breath and affirmations to support us through any spirals, and use boundaries and creative strategies to manage our time and energy, we will be well on the way to winning the war – not just the battle – against anxiety.

In some cases, anxiety may become a diagnosable disorder, which should be managed by a medical or mental health professional.

Hack

Anxiety is just a fancy word for firing up our body's warning system.

Check in

How much is anxiety contributing to my avoidance?

Self-talk

I am in control of my mind and body.

The Work

Set boundaries, practise saying no, create an achievable schedule, try grounding techniques, practise breath work, meditation and mindfulness, engage in physical activity, build in rest.

Core Beliefs

Our core beliefs are the blueprint for the way we experience the world. They create the lens through which we see ourselves and determine how we feel and respond to the people in our lives. This can work in our favour if we have positive core beliefs, but things can get a bit sticky when we are influenced by negative core beliefs. If we *believe* we don't deserve the good things that might be coming our way, we may not take the opportunities that appear in front of us. Similarly, when we are holding onto negative core beliefs, we might not even be aware that making a change in our lives, in any capacity, is even an option for us.

Identifying what core beliefs we might be bound by can be a daunting task. Often, we aren't even consciously aware that they exist, and it can take a healthy dose of reflection, by holding up that sometimes awfully confronting mirror, to understand what some of our early wiring might have done to our perception of ourselves and the world.

A good place to start might be in the landscape of your relationships with friends or family and how you respond to them. Have you ever found yourself deeply wounded when someone changes arrangements at the last minute, even though you felt entirely justified at the time? Or feeling betrayed when a friend doesn't agree with you? What happens when you experience a failure – is it a complete shock or does it feel entirely expected? Chances are, whichever way you lean, it may have something to do with your core beliefs.

In fact, our core beliefs can be the reason we are attracting the wrong relationships, staying in jobs that don't fulfil us or even maintaining friendships that might not be healthy or are no longer aligned with who we are. There are many reasons why we might be feeling like we're not good enough or that we feel unworthy, unlovable or undeserving of the things that come our way. How we evaluate ourselves and our place in the world comes from deep within our ingrained core beliefs that shape and define our perspective. In turn, this can be the very reason we decide not to take the leap when it comes to exploring our passions and interests or even begin to consider a new direction.

The good news is, we can change the way we think and, as a result, change the way we feel.

Early Childhood

It sounds like a cliché, but our early years shape us in every way imaginable. Our responses and values begin to generate all the way back through the relationships we have with our caregivers. If we are raised feeling loved and secure, then usually we go into the world feeling confident about who we are and how we fit in. When our start to life has been a bit rocky, it can often translate into difficulty with the way we see ourselves and our value.

Having a rocky childhood or a complicated relationship with our caregivers does not determine our outcome, however. It is helpful, though, to understand how much of our childhood experience influences and colours our adult world.

Take Layne Beachley as an example. When she learned as a child that she was adopted, she formed the core belief that she was unlovable. But instead of allowing that to influence her in a negative way, she used it as a driving force to achieve greatness. In her mind, she needed to become a world champion to be loved unconditionally. That was at the heart of what she was doing and why she pushed herself so hard from such a young age. Surfing, for Layne, was an ever-changing landscape that threw her all kinds of obstacles that challenged her from a physical and mental perspective. Instead of shrinking into herself, Layne was able to seize those moments and opportunities and turn them into gold.

She could have chosen to let the pain at the root of her belief dictate the terms of her life and this could very well have led her to an entirely different outcome. But by transforming that core belief into positive energy and not allowing it to define her, Layne completely changed the trajectory of her life.

We can all do the same thing by challenging the core beliefs that might be holding us back and preventing us from reaching our potential. But first, we have to reveal them.

Thoughts Versus Feelings

Identifying our own core beliefs takes some deep reflection and analysis of our responses to the people and situations we find ourselves in. We might find that we are resistant to new endeavours but are not quite sure why. We also might find that we have incredibly strong feelings about people or situations without even realising that they are preventing us from moving forward.

Our feelings can get very muddy at times and can be difficult to work through. It's not always immediately clear where the response is coming from and it takes patience and compassion to work through. The process of peeling back the layers can feel like we are completely out of control and that we're skidding down the freeway with only a handbrake to cling onto. It can be a pretty daunting experience when we don't know where our emotional responses are coming from, especially when they are impacting our lives in a negative way. And the notion of having to lift the lid on these unknown sources of distress can feel utterly terrifying. I often have clients disclose that they're afraid that, by unpacking the past and revealing the source of their distress, they will open the floodgates and not be able to take control of their emotions again. But, if it's done carefully, it doesn't have to be as scary as it might seem. It's important to remember that we can always regain control of our emotional responses and return to a place of safety. Part of that process is becoming comfortable with being uncomfortable.

Identifying our own
core beliefs takes
some deep reflection
and analysis of
our responses to
the people and
situations we find
ourselves in.

Our thoughts and our feelings create the roadmap for our interactions with others and our responses to the events and circumstances in our lives. If we're feeling like we're out of control, or losing direction, we should always refer back to that roadmap and perhaps alter course.

To do this, we first need to understand that our thoughts and our feelings are two distinct constructs. In fact, our thoughts are actually the gateway to our feelings. When we *think* about ourselves in a particular way, for example, as helpless or unlovable, we *feel* helpless and unlovable.

How often have you told yourself something and believed it? More often than you probably realise. At this point, perhaps it would be helpful to borrow a phrase from a highly controversial former US president and remind yourself that a lot of the negative press you give yourself is fake news!

In my experience as a therapist, we often see the greatest transformation once we have drilled down to find what is working against us, what is holding us back. So, pick up that drill, grab the torch and drop down into the mine shaft. Take note of the language you use with yourself. What is the narrative that you've been working with? Acknowledge the sticky parts that make you feel uncomfortable and walk right through them. Start filling your loot bag with the phrases and convictions you've had about yourself that may no longer serve you. Stacking them up alongside each other will help to give you the full picture of the identity your core beliefs have contributed to creating.

Have you ever told yourself that you could never apply for that job because you just wouldn't get it? Sadly, this is much more common among women than men. We have a tendency to believe our skills are not as desirable or that we need to check off every single key selection criterion before we'll even consider applying. Men, more often than not, will apply regardless of the number of skills they possess. It's interesting to consider the narrative that has been created in both cases: an adamant belief that it's not even worth trying versus self-belief that they are just as worthy and deserving as the next person. Food for thought.

Once we recognise that our thoughts are not facts, we release ourselves from the power of those thoughts. We can tell ourselves, 'I am worthy and capable (and I'm going to write a kick-ass cover letter explaining why these people should employ me, even without meeting all of the key selection criteria)'. We can tell ourselves, 'I deserve to explore my passions and try new things'. The more we think it, the more we believe it and the more positive we feel about ourselves.

The Big Impact

A belief, as defined in cognitive behaviour therapy, is a deeply ingrained, chronically practised thought. These ingrained thoughts – beliefs – can be about ourselves, about other people or about the world. Although they often form in our childhood, they can also form in young adulthood and be reinforced by experiences we might have.

When I worked in child protection, it was my job to investigate notifications of abuse and neglect and, in liaison with my team leader, make decisions about the safety of a child, which would often include removing them from their home. It was an incredibly difficult job, and I take my hat off to those who stay in the role long term. I was there for just over a year before burning out. In those short 14 months, and as a pretty green recent psychology graduate, I might add, I saw things that drastically changed my view of the world. It left such an impression on me that for many years afterwards, I had a warped perspective of men, in particular. In one instance, when a neighbour had been talking with my father and me outside our house, I became incredibly uncomfortable after noticing him stroking his son affectionately. I sprang into work mode and immediately made assumptions about the father, leaping to negative conclusions. When I voiced my concerns to my dad, he laughed and told me that he had observed a perfectly natural and loving interaction between father and son, and that perhaps I needed to consider the impact that my work was having on my perspective. I was shocked by his response and indeed at mine, compelling me to re-examine my judgement and remember that it was in fact entirely possible that not all men were paedophiles and abusers.

As trite as that may seem, that moment was an eye-opener for me. It was the first time I had become aware that my core beliefs had changed and were clouding my perspective entirely. My experience of the world had been altered by the complexity of the work I was doing, at a time when I was still quite vulnerable and professionally naive.

It was only after I left that role that I was able to reintegrate my childhood core beliefs about safety and family, and recalibrate my view of the world.

What Can You Do About It?

Negative core beliefs can impact our self-esteem and self-worth, and limit our ability to adapt and bounce back. To change unhelpful core beliefs, the first step is recognising when they occur. Keep a journal or make a note of the self-talk you use throughout the day. Are you reacting to situations or conversations in a big way? What kind of thoughts do you have about yourself? Have you noticed any themes in your thinking? Once you have identified any negative patterns of thinking or automatic thoughts, counteract them with a positive. Collect evidence of the positives and write them down, then celebrate them. The more we notice and celebrate the opposite of these negative patterns of thinking, the more we believe them.

It's important to acknowledge that this may be a slow process. While shifting your perspective is key to changing core beliefs, it may take some time to overcome any automatic thoughts. Thinking you're not good enough, that you shouldn't apply for that role, that you could never try that thing – those are automatic negative thoughts that, once addressed, can transform into thoughts such as I *can* do that, I'll throw my hat in the ring and see what happens, I deserve good things.

Spend some time identifying those core beliefs, then pour your energy and focus into strengthening the new positive core beliefs. By rewiring your perspective, you are changing the lens through which you see yourself and the world.

Hack

Core beliefs are not fixed. We can change the way we view ourselves and the world.

Check in

What are the negative automatic thoughts I'm having about myself?

Self-talk

I can transform my thoughts and, in turn, my feelings about myself and my place in the world.

The Work

Identify any negative patterns of thought and replace them with positive ones. Don't believe the hype – you are not your automatic thoughts. Reflection may take time, and challenging, then shifting, these unhelpful beliefs will not happen overnight. Be kind to yourself as you embark on this phase of investigation and tackle one belief at a time.

Perfectionism

Some of the most successful people in the world attribute their success to perfectionism. It is often regarded as a highly desirable personality trait, with the belief that the highest level of performance can be expected from that person. The greatest athletes in the world talk about having to maintain a level of perfectionism to achieve the success that they have. And some of the most celebrated musicians, performers and tech giants at the top of their game have made the same connection.

Employers might think this is exactly what they're looking for in a potential employee, assuming anyone with perfectionism listed as a professional quality will be a hardworking, tenacious go-getter who won't stand for anything less than precision. It might create a hint of competition among colleagues or in friendships – *she's a perfectionist, so she does things better than you.*

It could be used as a humble brag in a job interview when asked to describe what you might need to work on. The inference being that, really, it's one of your strengths and your potential employer can look forward to reaping the benefits of your laser-like focus and dedication to tasks. If only you didn't care so much about doing the best job. Sigh.

But what if I told you that true perfectionism actually does more harm than good? Would you be surprised?

Having a low level of perfectionism or positive perfectionism can actually be a good thing and may be what drives those well-known hall-of-famers. Positive perfectionism often presents as high motivation and drive, and a strong desire to achieve and to succeed. However, what we know about high levels of perfectionism and, in particular, negative perfectionism is that it often has a significant detrimental effect on mental health.

Not So Perfect After All

One of the traits that we see in perfectionism is the tendency to set exceedingly high expectations that most often cannot be met. This usually goes hand in hand with having highly critical beliefs about yourself and of how others perceive you, as well as difficulty accepting criticism and adapting to change.

In fact, rather than fostering high levels of achievement, it's very common for perfectionism to increase levels of procrastination and avoidance, which is part of the reason why it can be a barrier to change. Right alongside that stalling and delay can be a fear of failure that underlies the perfectionism. It's not always just about becoming the best, but rather avoiding the personal impact of failure, whether real or perceived.

Positive perfectionism often presents as high motivation and drive, and a strong desire to achieve and to succeed.

This very tangled web of self-defeat can have a significantly negative impact on mental health. Much of the research around perfectionism and mental health shows a direct correlation between true perfectionism and diagnoses such as depression, anxiety, eating disorders and obsessive-compulsive disorder (OCD). If we are constantly striving to be the best of the best and setting goals for ourselves that are not achievable, then the impact of that perceived failure can be devastating. In some cases, the personal expectations are so high that the wheels are perpetually spinning without any ability to launch. This can then become a vicious cycle of frustration and disappointment, which can become critical to a person's wellbeing.

One of the other ways that perfectionism can take a toll is in the inability to set boundaries. Sarah Davidson touched on this during our conversation (flip back to the Anxiety chapter to read more of her story there), sharing the impact that saying yes to everything can have on your mental health. If there's an expectation, whether set by yourself or by parents in childhood, that you must always excel in both your personal and professional life, this can become very challenging if you are doing well, but have an inability to say no and take your foot off the accelerator. This will very quickly lead to burnout, and the cycle of distress about a lack of perceived achievement or fear of failure begins again. Not to mention the physical and psychological impact of the burnout itself.

The Seeds of Perfection

Perfectionism is a trait that can develop over time as a result of our lived experiences and expectations, or it can be a trait we are born with. I have often wondered if this is what we see in some children who show some minor delays in their early years of development. For example, the child that sits back and takes it all in, watching and processing but not appearing to participate at all. Then suddenly, they demonstrate the skill quite masterfully out of nowhere. Perhaps language was a little delayed at first, then, as if out of nowhere, they're speaking quite clearly. Or they showed reluctance to get up onto their feet and make attempts at walking – then, out of nowhere, they've gone from crawling to walking quite confidently, completely skipping the practice and failure part. Are they waiting until they are sure they can do it *perfectly* before giving it a go?

In adults, it's a similar process for some perfectionists. We assume that it's a sign of success and achievement and that the high-flyers must be perfectionists to achieve greatness. And yes, there is some truth to that. But it does come at a cost. In many cases, perfectionism is actually the cause of major distress and disfunction and, as esteemed researcher Dr Brené Brown[3] puts it, is correlated with life paralysis and missed opportunities. Some perfectionists will be overwhelmed by the fear of failure, which leads to avoidance and anxiety, before the task or set goal is even attempted.

As you can see, there is a lot of focus on how things *should* be, what the outcome *should* be, rather than just launching in and giving it a go.

There are ways to overcome this, however, and it starts as simply as recognising the difference between having high standards and high motivation or drive and being a perfectionist. When your expectations of your performance in a task cause distress, anger, frustration or low mood to a point that it's interfering with your ability to complete the task, it might be that there is an issue with perfectionism. How much energy do you spend focusing on the details of a task or finding yourself refining your work to excess, never quite happy with the result? This can also be a sign that there is an issue with perfectionism.

Just Do It

To combat this, start to subscribe to the theory that done is better than perfect – words on the page, output that might not win awards, more achievable task lists. Reinforce that idea by practising being comfortable in the discomfort. The email wasn't perfect, but it was sent. The essay wasn't perfect, but it was pretty good. The job application wasn't perfect, but it hit the main points.

Changing the narrative in your own mind about what 'done' looks like means also having to shift the perspective on yourself. Start by treating yourself as you would treat a friend. When you complete a task, congratulate yourself on the effort you made, rather than looking for things to critique.

Try not to define your success by how well you might do something. The key is just to give something a go. When an opportunity arises, let go of the fourteen-page pros and cons list, don't look for mountains of evidence to substantiate throwing your hat into the ring, and release yourself from the focus on what others might think of you if you decide to try something new.

Challenge the thoughts that feed the perfectionism. This can feel like a tough habit to break; however, acknowledging that it's an issue and actively stopping the problematic thought or behaviour is already a big step towards breaking the cycle and relieving yourself of the pressure.

Remember that practice makes perfect (pardon the pun). The internal measure of success will take some time to recalibrate, so use that positive reframing that you're getting so good at now. Counter the negative thoughts about results and performance, judgement and criticism, with words that applaud attempts and effort.

Brown makes the link between perfectionism and shame, believing that, at its core, perfectionism is about trying to earn approval and that this in itself creates a dangerous and debilitating belief system. Look at ways you can create an alternate narrative that helps you to identify your strengths outside your achievements. Is there another way to feel good about yourself beyond your desire to prove yourself through accomplishments? To receive approval for who you are, not for what you do?

Turn the fear of failure into being brave, making bold moves and attempting things before you have all the pieces of the puzzle. Actively engage with the thought that good enough really is good enough in most scenarios. Then celebrate the checking of that box – done! Not necessarily perfect, but done. Tick.

Hack

Done is better than perfect. Attempting is better than failing.

Check in

How much pressure do you put on yourself to achieve at the highest level in your personal and professional life? How is that pressure impacting your mental health?

Self-talk

Good enough really is good enough.

The Work

To reduce procrastination, break your task list down into realistic, achievable goals. Practise positive self-talk that applauds your effort, rather than criticises the output. Set boundaries around social and professional expectations, and actively practise self-care. What can you do to release yourself from judgement?

Self-esteem

The term self-esteem is often used as an umbrella concept in reference to how we see ourselves, how we should feel about ourselves and what we could be working on. But what does it actually mean? In the media and across social-networking sites, self-esteem is talked about as a construct that needs to be improved or is seen as the reason behind personal failures. We are instructed to make this a priority when looking for ways to improve ourselves. We are encouraged to keep it in mind when thinking about how we raise our children and adolescents. In particular, self-esteem is a hot topic in relation to the development of our sense of identity and self-worth, especially for young women.

When we talk with our friends about someone who might be making poor choices or behaving in a particular way, we might make reference to their self-esteem. We have created a culture of acceptance with regard to celebrities who have normalised drastically altering their faces and bodies due to a lack of self-esteem. Even in the way we might judge a participant on our favourite reality TV series, the online commentary frequently boils down to a conversation about self-esteem. That cocky young guy who comes across as arrogant and irritating – he thinks too highly of himself. The young girl who appears weak or without self-respect – she doesn't think highly enough of herself.

While it's wonderful that there is now wider acknowledgement that behaviour is an indicator of an undercurrent of psychological responses, carving up our faces or enabling poor choices isn't necessarily the best way to approach it. Self-esteem is so much more than just an excuse for outrageous television antics and it's certainly not black and white either. It can be high or low and everything in between.

How we view ourselves or our value can impact our health and wellbeing, as well as our ability to propel ourselves forward in relationships, in our careers and in our own personal development. Crucially, it has a big impact on our decision-making ability.

Where Does Low Self-esteem Come From?

There are many factors that impact the development of self-esteem. Like most things, it can begin in childhood. The early experiences we have and the interactions with the important people in our lives are a big part of what shapes our concept of ourselves and our value within that. It can also be affected by relationships and friendships that may not have been healthy. In the workplace, having a manager or a colleague who doesn't treat us with respect can have an impact on the way we see and value ourselves. There may be events that have transpired in our personal lives that make us more vulnerable in other situations, which will then have an impact on our self-esteem.

We commonly hear about self-esteem in the context of body-image issues and in the way we might behave in a relationship. But the issues arising from low self-esteem can present in other ways too.

Think about how we might behave at work or within our friendships. How we relate to others and what we allow into our personal and professional spaces is an indicator of how we might be feeling about ourselves. Low self-esteem can look like people-pleasing, difficulty creating or maintaining firm boundaries, hypersensitivities, difficulty in bouncing back from challenges or setbacks, being more critical of ourselves or others, and being less confident in decision-making.

Having all of that swirling around in the background, while trying to find the courage to chase a new dream or follow a new direction, can certainly make things challenging and complex. It might feel like things are out of reach and inhibit us to the point where we won't even dare consider the possibility.

Self-esteem or Confidence?

One of the biggest misconceptions about self-esteem is that if we have low self-esteem, we have low confidence and that we feel that way across all the facets of our lives. That's not entirely true. We can still have confidence in a particular area of our lives, while also living with low self-esteem.

A perfect example of this is something the lovely Olivia Rogers shared with me during our interview for *The Curious Life* podcast in 2019. Olivia is a former Miss Universe Australia who has publicly shared her battle with body image and disordered eating. At the height of her illness, she was achieving more than most people do in a lifetime. Outwardly, she appeared to be a self-assured, outgoing, totally together young woman at the top of her game. She was a successful model, was completing a speech pathology degree and was living what many would assume was an enviable life. Meanwhile, underneath it all, she described feeling the after-effects of her parents' divorce as a young child, and the impact of the constant remarks from industry professionals about her weight and appearance taking a toll.

Remarkably, Olivia was able to excel in her studies at university, while suffering privately through the darkest depths of an eating disorder. She described having panic attacks and suicidal thoughts and yet, still, was able to sit her exams and turn up to photo shoots and maintain the facade of someone who was succeeding in all the various components of her life. In this way, Olivia was able to utilise her confidence in her academic and professional abilities to perform well, despite the fact that her self-esteem was at an all-time low and was manifesting in significant physical and mental illness.

While this is an extreme example, and one that shows what an incredible and tenacious young woman Olivia is, it highlights the reality that confidence and self-esteem are not one and the same.

Self-esteem in Relationships

Do you ever look back at past relationships and wonder 'why did I stay in that situation for so long?' Or 'what did I see in that person?' Perhaps you're in that position now. Sometimes it can be a bit of a chicken-and-egg scenario – did I come into this relationship with low self-esteem or did the relationship slowly eat away at it? Each relationship can provide us with valuable lessons and prepare us for the next chapter of our lives. Unfortunately, like so many things, it's often only with the benefit of hindsight that we work out what the purpose of that relationship was and what the lessons were.

When we come into a relationship with low self-esteem, whether that is from a complicated childhood or wounds we may not have fully healed from, we can bring those patterns of thought and behaviour with us. Some of that will protect us and some might prevent us from moving forward.

All of our past experiences do actually serve a purpose. Whether we realise it or not, those sticky situations and uncomfortable conversations are the breeding ground for growth and development.

In my own life, I remember a short relationship I had been in that, with hindsight, was entirely and utterly wrong. The relationship materialised after a significant period of singledom and probably came at a time when, despite looking like I had things pretty well together, certainly from a professional point of view, in fact, my self-esteem could have done with a bit of a boost. This relationship came along and was thrust at me on a silver platter full of enthusiasm, which, as anyone who has ever been single for a long period of time will know, can be a very rare and bamboozling gem. After many years of wondering if that special someone would find their way into my orbit, this someone did. Although the relationship burned through quickly and became abundantly clear that it was not the right fit, on reflection, it was a challenging step in the right direction, preparing me for the next stage of my relationship constellation.

Personally, I wasn't sure the relationship had been a good idea or worthwhile, but, with time and through lengthy discussions with friends, I could see that developmentally it was an important move on the chessboard. It helped me to rebuild some of the self-esteem that had receded and eroded after a long time on my own and showed me that I deserved something different. The lesson was in working out what I wanted from a relationship and being ready for that when it eventually arrived. In doing that work, I was letting go of old patterns of thinking and beliefs that no longer served me.

It would have been easy for me to look at that failed relationship and question myself about how and why I ended up entangled with someone that was so wrong for me. However, it's a bit of a slippery slope to look back on choices and beat yourself up for them. If we can take the failures and the mismatches and the dead ends in our stride and use them as an opportunity to grow and learn, then nothing is a waste of time. Nothing is futile. We are just moving towards the next great thing and we need to be ready and open to receive it.

Self-esteem and Self-worth

Despite sounding like similar ideas, there is an important distinction between these two concepts. Self-esteem is how we see ourselves and our place in the world, and this is often confused with self-worth. Our self-worth is a much more introspective concept. It is literally about how *worthy* we feel internally in all aspects of our lives – worthy of love, worthy of respect, worthy of belonging, worthy of just being.

Again, like so many things, our level of self-worth can be a consequence of our experiences from childhood, from relationships and from life circumstances that shape our beliefs about our value.

This is a tricky one, because in order to improve our self-esteem, we need to believe we are worthy of this improvement. When we feel worthy of the things we deserve, this has a positive impact on our mental and physical wellbeing as well as on our drive and motivation. This, in turn, has a flow-on effect to our ability to make decisions to move forward and make the most of opportunities that come our way.

So, What Can We Do About It?

Evaluating Priorities

Take a moment to consider the boundaries that might be blurred for you. Do you say yes when you really mean no? Are you the last person to leave a social gathering, even though you're tired and need to go home? Do you offer to help others consistently, while your own needs are being overlooked? If the answer is yes to any of these questions, be assured that you're absolutely not alone.

Think about your energy reserves as a cup filled with water; pour some out for work, some for social life and some for family. There may be other obligations or areas of your life that also need a little pour. The trick is to ensure there is enough of that precious liquid in that cup for yourself, before all your responsibilities have been met. If you're pouring all your energy into the things or the people that don't serve you, or emptying your cup before you've even had a sip, then you may need to rethink your priorities. Giving yourself permission to put yourself at the top of the priority list is the first step to building up your self-esteem.

Other Ways to Improve

Boosting your self-esteem may feel like an intimidating task at first, but start simply by creating a list of your strengths. Alongside that, add the things you would like to improve on. As you work through the list, be kind to yourself and try to remember that this is a long game. Even just refining the way that you speak to yourself and think about yourself can go a long way towards improving your self-esteem. The more we say it, the more we believe it, so become your own champion and cheer yourself on from the sidelines, and remember that any perceived failure is only a part of the lesson.

One way to keep track of your progress is by keeping a journal. I realise there may be many an eye roll in reading that, but, for those who connect with writing and visualising the things we are working on, a journal is a tangible place to collect the evidence that helps to build up our arsenal of strengths and positive beliefs about ourselves. Spoil yourself with some beautiful stationery and make it a joyful experience – a place where you counteract negative thoughts with positive ones, engage in creativity and remind yourself of the qualities that will carry you forward into the next phase of your life as you embrace change.

Boosting your
self-esteem
may feel like an
intimidating task at
first, but start simply
by creating
a list of your
strengths.

While we have talked a lot about low self-esteem here, if you're reading this and thinking it doesn't apply, then you might be one of the lucky ones with healthy self-esteem. If that's the case, perhaps you could consider the ways you might be able to support the people around you to weather their own storms and create their new boundaries. Not only will that continue to improve your own self-esteem, but it can mean the difference between a good and a bad day for someone you care about.

Hack

Self-esteem is about how we see and value ourselves and our place in the world.

Check in

How is my self-esteem impacting my drive and relationships? How firm are my boundaries and do I need to say no more often? What language am I using when I look in the mirror or think about myself?

Self-talk

I am good enough. I deserve everything that I want in life.

The Work

Treat yourself as you would treat a friend – with endless kindness and support. Quash those negative thoughts with positive ones and make a commitment to changing the narrative you have created for yourself. Celebrate your wins and achievements, no matter how small, and remind yourself each day of the things you like about yourself.

Fear

We've spent some time looking at some of the psychological reasons behind our resistance to change, most of them relating to the issues that may stem from childhood or experiences we've had along the way. However, the biggest barrier to change is most often fear.

When I was talking to people about the subject of this book and asking what they thought held them back from seizing opportunities and taking a chance on change, unequivocally, the answer was fear. Fear is something that we all feel and there is no shame in that.

In fact, social media is littered with artwork and memes urging us to 'feel the fear and do it anyway' – to be scared and push through it. I've been guilty of using similar quotes and language to encourage people to take those leaps in life too. But it's never quite as simple as that.

Normalising fear is important, but there could be many reasons why we're frightened of change. We might be worrying about the outcome, anxious about decision-making, or perhaps we're concerned about whether we will lose something by taking the next step in our lives. Afraid to succeed. Afraid to take risks. Afraid to fail. Some people stay in relationships they've outgrown, in houses that don't quite fit their needs anymore and in jobs that are no longer fulfilling them. Perhaps we tell ourselves 'I could never ...' when thinking about trying something new or that we're secretly wishing we could do. Why? Because the alternative can feel too scary.

So, what is it about fear that compels us to override our actual needs and wants?

The fear of putting ourselves out there and taking a risk is powerful. When we are frightened or feel fear, our amygdala becomes activated. It's the part of the brain that is involved in emotion and behaviour, and is known for its significant role in our fear responses. A little bit of fear is a good thing, just like anxiety. A little nudge from our internal warning system to be alert and be aware. Too much fear and we can become stuck, reactive or triggered.

One of the best descriptions of how this works is from psychologist Daniel Goleman.[4] He coined the phrase 'amygdala hijacking' to explain what happens when we lose control or experience an intense or immediate emotional reaction that's out of proportion to the situation. If you're a parent you will no doubt be able to recount a plethora of examples of when you've lost your cool after a busy morning and the kids aren't listening, or perhaps you've exploded at your partner when they've unwittingly triggered your anxiety by asking a simple request of you when it's all just too much – the straw that broke the camel's back. It's almost as if the gasket just blows, no matter how rational you may have been in the moments leading up to it.

Although we would expect to see this in someone who has experienced trauma, the amygdala hijack is also a common response to chronic stress and overwhelm. This response evolved in our early development as human beings – it's a vital fear response imperative to survival. At that time, it was the animal-like response that we might have experienced in the face of a real threat to our lives. It's this hijacking that triggers the fight-or-flight response and shuts down our ability to respond rationally to the situation. Today, it can look like an irrational emotional outburst that is often the result of feeling frazzled, swamped or not coping – an archaic response to a thoroughly modern affliction.

According to Goleman, an amygdala hijacking has three parts to it; a strong emotional response, then sudden activation, followed by the realisation that the response was inappropriate.

For anyone who has been a parent to young children, this will probably sound very familiar. Pick up your toys. Put on your shoes. Stop hitting your brother. Be gentle, please. Put on your shoes. Please put that down. We need to go. Don't empty that drawer, please. You're going to break that. Object breaks. *EXPLOSION*. Then, the subsequent guilt for having shouted at your little people who have no impulse control and only partially developed brains. Even though your own reaction might have made it appear that you too have no impulse control and a partially developed brain, we know that's not the case.

What has happened is the rational part of the brain has been overtaken by a biological response, causing us to react irrationally. Because it wasn't just about the interaction with the kids, or the broken object; it's the cumulative stress building up – the burden of other responsibilities looming and your mind being in three different places at once. All of these pressures culminating in a colossal brain snap that, for a brief moment, renders us out of control.

So how do we control the irrational response to a perceived threat while we are stressed? By recognising the signals and triggers that occur in the body right before we react. If we imagine the case of the beleaguered parent in the previous example, the first thing they might look at is whether they notice their anger starting to build in the lead-up to the explosion, through physical sensations. Is their heart rate rising? Has their breathing changed? Is there a change in their body temperature or have they suddenly become aware of their firmly clamped jaw? When our amygdala is triggered, it floods our system with cortisol and adrenaline – our stress hormone and our fight-or-flight response. In our previous evolutionary state this would have served us well, launching us into the fight or flight for our life. For us very evolved present-day humans, our children maddeningly ignoring us as we're trying to gather belongings and bustle them out the door isn't necessarily life-threatening. However, it can very much trigger that same response, and those are the signs to watch for.

Fearing Change?

In a subtle or overt way, this can be the same response that occurs in our bodies when we imagine taking a risk or putting ourselves in perceived danger. The notion of leaving a relationship can trigger that very response, as can shifting gears entirely on your career trajectory or contemplating a move.

When you think about making a change in your life, take a moment to notice whether some of those same responses occur in your own body. Do you think about changing your career path and suddenly feel your heart palpitate or a rush of blood surging through your body? That doesn't mean that it's the wrong decision or the wrong path to take, it just might feel scary. The warning system went off. Notice that reaction and ask yourself what might be underlying the response. Examine the evidence that does or does not support the reaction and ask yourself whether there might be another way to look at it.

There are many reasons that we might go scurrying back to our comfort zone and pull the blankets tightly over our heads – some that are created out of our own sense of shoulds and shouldn'ts and others for more tangible reasons.

The global pandemic in itself has been a genuine source of fear for so many of us, and for very good reason. There has been and still continues to be a very real risk of illness and even worse for the vulnerable people in our community, for the people we love, for ourselves. Our way of life has been threatened, turned upside down and has thrown us from the dizzying heights of uncertainty and back. It is entirely reasonable to expect that some of us will need more time than others to emerge from this thrashing.

However, it is important to try to recover our strength bit by bit and to regain control of our lives and our choices. Acknowledging our fear is one thing, and feeling it is entirely acceptable, but allowing it to dictate the terms of our lives is another thing altogether. If you have been impacted by the global pandemic, as a result of a business loss, cancelled weddings, repeated lockdowns and isolation, or through illness or the loss of someone you love, fear may be a big part of your experience right now.

Global pandemic or not, if you find that fear is the dominating factor in your life affecting your decision-making at present, there are ways to gradually move yourself through that.

First, you may need to do some work on grief or anxiety, but alongside that there is plenty you can do to overcome fear. Start by setting a small goal each day to push yourself outside of your comfort zone. Is there one thing each day that you can achieve to build up a repertoire of wins? Perhaps it's as simple as going for a walk or setting a reasonable exercise schedule. Double points there, as it not only helps you feel you've achieved something, but exercise, as we know, is very much a prescription for a range of mental health concerns. Can you push yourself a little further socially? Interact with friends by

If you find
that fear is the
dominating factor in
your life affecting your
decision-making at
present, there are ways
to gradually move
yourself through it.

phone rather than just through text. Build your confidence in your ability to communicate and connect again after such a strange time in the world.

There might be opportunities to dip your toes into a dream project or a creative outlet that you've been thinking about trying. Again, start small – even just searching on the internet and investigating a bit more about what is involved in that project or new experience you'd like to try is a step forward in itself.

Each activity that you set and achieve acts as a benchmark to measure your progress against. The aim is to gradually increase your accomplishments, to rebuild a sense of strength, control and purpose in your life again.

For many of us, it's much easier to stay well and truly inside our safety zone. A place where we can be content with what we have and where we are in life, even if it's not exactly where our passion lies. That might be enough for many of us. But if the global pandemic has taught us anything it's that life is for the taking. We lose nothing by trying something new (unless we're thinking about adding extreme sports to our roster, that is!). Perhaps this global reset has granted us the permission to choose something new for ourselves, to live the lives that we deserve.

So, what will you choose? Fight, flight or freeze?

Hack

Fear is a normal part of life, but it doesn't have to be prohibitive.

Check in

How is fear impacting your life from a social, emotional and behavioural perspective?

Self-talk

I can do this. I deserve this.

The Work

Set small tasks that push you out of your comfort zone, and gradually increase the frequency and the challenge. Examine your self-talk and rewire those thoughts. If you're talking yourself out of opportunities, engagements or exploration, tell yourself you *can* do those things. Think through the worst-case scenario and compare that to the likely outcome of the risk you're thinking about taking. Anticipation is always scarier than reality. Dare to be brave.

Ego

You might think that ego is one of the big obstructions to change and you may be right, but not strictly for the reasons you might be thinking. It's not uncommon to hear negative comments about someone having a big ego or having let their ego get in the way of something, implying that they're arrogant or self-absorbed. But having an ego is not quite the flawed personality trait it's been made out to be. In fact, it's a vital part of our personality that is required to help steady our course.

The term 'ego' has become muddied over the years as it has made its way out of psychological textbooks and into the mainstream. It has taken on a very different interpretation than the one that the godfather of psychoanalysis, Dr Sigmund Freud, first described in his early years of psychoanalytic theory.

When Freud identified ego as a part of our personality development, he didn't intend for it to be featured as a solo act, but, rather, very much as a stabilising force between warring performers in the trio act of our minds. He proposed that there are three parts to our personality that we acquire at different times in our development – the id, the ego and the superego.

The general idea is that the id is responsible for the primitive and instinctive impulses and urges that drive us. These operate under the pleasure principle, meaning these are needs that seek to be met immediately, regardless of the consequences. If left to its own devices, our id would have us seeking instant gratification at all times, rendering us victims to our animal instincts.

The superego is at the other end of the spectrum and is dictated by the values and morals of society, beginning with those ingrained in us by our parents. Our parental values and the social world around us play a big part in the development of our superego, creating the first building blocks of social expectations that then impact our decision-making in later years. If the superego reigned supreme, we would likely live very narrow lives full of judgement and high morality.

Our ego, as defined by Freud, is the moral middle ground, playing mediator between the instant-gratification wants of the id and the rules and expectations of the superego. The ego operates under the reality principle, finding ways to serve the needs of the id through careful consideration, making calculated, realistic moves to avoid negative consequences. It is not at all the maniacal narcissist we imagine when discussing ego.

Freud described the id as the horse and the ego as the rider, trying to hold in check the superior strength of the horse.[5] So, the ego is not the one that's out of control in the scenarios that we imagine these days; it is in fact the id that might be needing a tighter rein. If our ego is underdeveloped, we may find ourselves beholden to social or parental expectations or perhaps being driven by our primal instincts, rather than being able to take measured steps towards a positive direction.

Having a healthy ego, from a psychological perspective, means not over- or under-estimating ourselves or our abilities or achievements.

Developmental psychologist Erik Erikson[6] took Freud's theories a little further, describing ego as necessary for establishing and maintaining identity, being incredibly adaptive and being closely linked to mental health. He described a weaker ego as having a lack of direction, feeling unproductive and not having a strong sense of identity. All of these are incredibly important in terms of taking charge of our lives and grasping opportunities as they arise.

Many of the great theorists have interpreted ego in their own way and the concept has evolved in numerous ways. Developmental psychologist Jean Piaget[7] used egocentrism to describe the tunnel-vision perspective that children have of themselves. The way they see themselves as the centre of the universe, with difficulty imagining alternative perspectives. This is more in line with the modern-day use of the term ego when it's used to describe someone who might be self-centred or perceived as focused on being the best, the most admired or being overly motivated.

Work Out What Is Holding You Back

So why is all of this psychobabble important? Because sometimes we need to be reminded to get out of our own way – to find alignment with who we are, what we want and our expression of need. We will each have a different interpretation of ego and our place in the world, just as the founding voices of psychological theory have had. It's our job to reflect on what's important to us and to find a way to dial up the parts of ourselves that deserve to be heard and dial down the parts that don't serve us.

If you sit quietly with your own thoughts for a moment, where do you truly want to be? Is it at home with a family? Is it running a company? Is it helping others? Drown out the white noise, the imposter syndrome, the anxiety and the self-doubt and run towards the thing that deep down you know you're aching to do. Reach for that goal, bit by bit.

One way to do that is to become vulnerable with yourself. The walls that we build up to protect ourselves can feel like they've taken up permanent real estate in our minds. Nothing is permanent. Nothing is fixed. Bring in the wrecking ball and knock those bricks right down. Be honest with yourself about who you are and what brings you joy. You absolutely do not need to share this with anyone else, particularly in the exploration phase, but it's incredibly important to get real with yourself.

Part of being vulnerable with yourself is accepting that there will be some things we don't know and that perhaps the next step in our path is unclear. And that is okay. The important part is listening to that inner child and discovering who that little person really is, underneath all those defences and excuses we make for ourselves.

It can be quite confronting to strip back the layers and look so deeply inward, but, by giving ourselves the opportunity for stillness and personal exploration, we can uncover gems that can transform our lives. You might discover why you have been feeling stuck or that there are avenues of exploration you hadn't yet given yourself permission to admit. You might find that you've been defensive or reactive in response to particular people or situations and, by taking the time to sit with it and remove the judgement from it, you can begin to understand why it is that you're behaving that way and carry out some repairs.

Moving through our insecurities and self-doubt helps us to build a healthy ego, in the traditional definition of the word. Freud's original description of ego was in German, described as *ich*, meaning *I*. It was then translated to English and given the Latin word *ego* to make it sound more scientific. In a way, this altered the true meaning of Freud's theory so that the concepts began to be clouded. However, if we think about building a healthy ego from the perspective of *I*, we can work towards bringing ourselves back to who we are at the core, what we want and where we need to go.

If you are already clear about who you are and where you want to go, spend some time on what has prevented you from doing that so far. Is it the expectations of the people who are important to you that have held you back? Are there societal norms that you're adhering to, whether consciously or unconsciously? Where is the pressure coming from?

If you're unclear of your next steps or what your next direction might look like, peel back the layers and try to visualise what would make you happiest. Nothing is too big or too small; it's just a matter of being honest with yourself about your truest desires.

Hack

Redefine ego as a good thing, the centre of your being.

Check in

Who are you at your core? What has been preventing you from accessing that point?

Self-talk

I give myself permission to explore the things I truly desire.

The Work

Practise being vulnerable. Treat yourself with compassion and release yourself from judgement. Spend some time with yourself, behind the layers of complexity and the protective self-made walls. Accept that it may not always feel comfortable, but that there's power in the uncomfortable. Push yourself beyond your comfort zone and try new things. Explore your thoughts and feelings honestly, through journalling or in other ways that help you express yourself. When you're feeling brave, share these thoughts and new discoveries with someone you trust.

Anger

Nothing gets us stuck in our feelings quite like anger does. It's a sticky mess of triggers and responses, conscious or not, that can sometimes lead us down paths we may not like.

Having said that, anger really does get a bad rap. There can be a lot of shame associated with anger that has shrouded it in negativity and labelled it as a dirty feeling or bad reaction. We blame bad behaviour on anger as if it's an unacceptable human response.

In reality, we all experience anger and, in most cases, it is a healthy and often very useful emotion. All the way across the spectrum from mild irritation and frustration to full-blown rage, there are many factors that influence the level of reaction we might have. Depending on the day or the event, these can range from environmental stressors and situational triggers to historical events that may have left us with a wound that is easily activated.

When we're holding onto pain or hurt, or perhaps a sense of betrayal or a feeling that we may have been wronged in some way, this can trigger an anger response that, in turn, can have a negative impact on our wellbeing and ability to move forward. In some cases, anger is absolutely warranted and, if expressed in a healthy way, can be quite cathartic.

Unfortunately, though, when we stay in that feeling and let it fester, it can direct us to cut off our noses to spite our faces. This is rarely a conscious decision. Staying in our anger is usually less to do with the actual event or interaction and more about what's bubbling away under the surface. When anger is the dominant feeling that is causing us distress and impacting our lives in a negative way, we need to look at the underlying cause.

Anger is almost always a secondary response to another emotion. If we can address the principal feeling, for example, grief, anxiety, hurt or betrayal, we can regain control of the anger response. This can take quite a bit of reflection as it's highly unlikely we will be aware of what is lying beneath our anger in the heat of the moment. Superficially, of course, we might think we know why we're triggered, maybe realising that we feel misunderstood by someone or rejected. But once the dust has settled and the Hulk has receded, this is when it would be helpful to do a little personal investigation as to what the true root of the issue might be.

Anger is almost always a secondary response to another emotion. If we can address the principal feeling, we can regain control of the anger response.

Peeling the Onion

Taking rejection as an example, if we have been upset by the ending of a relationship, are we angry because that person has chosen to move on? Or are we responding like that because we feel hurt that they no longer see a future with us? Perhaps we are grieving the loss of the future we anticipated or feel humiliated about the way that it ended. None of these examples are mutually exclusive, of course, and having more layers to the loss will add weight to the response.

Going through one or more experiences like this can sometimes be enough for a person to say 'I'm done with dating', in either the short or long term. And when that happens, the anger has won and we have cut off our nose to spite our face.

The same can be applied to many other circumstances. If our parents have expectations that we should follow a certain career path, for example, and this is not where our interests lie, that can create an incredible amount of frustration and pent-up emotion. We might feel angry that our parents are pressuring us into an industry we have no desire for, but what are we really feeling? Are we hurt that our parents are more invested in their own interests than ours? That their agenda is more important to them than our feelings? Maybe we feel rejected by them or sense that we are experiencing conditional love? Perhaps their expectations feel unfair or unjust, or are complicated by tricky family dynamics.

All of these complex and many-layered feelings are often expressed as anger and, instead of moving through the primary feelings, we can get stuck in our anger, which makes identifying or accepting new opportunities much more difficult.

Moving Through the Roots

Grief is one of those myriad primary emotions that can trigger anger within us.

In my time at the Coroners Court, I frequently encountered rage in grieving people. I have personally experienced it too. When we lose someone we love suddenly or without warning, the pain and injustice of the loss can quite easily transform into anger. This can be something we inflict upon many an unsuspecting person, who just happens to be in the wrong place at the wrong time.

My first victim of misplaced rage was the well-meaning hospital receptionist, just trying to do her job, as we gathered in the lobby, just moments after my mother had passed away. I had taken out my phone and was responding to a message from a relative, when the staff member politely informed me that phones were not to be used inside the hospital. You can imagine how well that went down. Although I spared that innocent clerk the direct wrath of my response, I certainly made my feelings clear as I barked out incoherent sentences into the air around me about my mother just having died. I was hyper-aware of the uncomfortable eyebrows arching in my direction in the waiting room, but, in that moment, I just didn't care. Not being able to use my phone for three minutes was absolutely not what I was angry about.

I noticed that anger stayed with me for some time, silently frothing away under the surface, finding myself easily enraged about things that didn't deserve that much heat. At the time, I was sure I was angry for the reason in front of me, but with the benefit of time I can see that much of that rapid activation was due to the suffering I was experiencing from the loss.

Similarly, it wasn't uncommon for some of my clients at the Coroners Court to engage in complaints about the coronial process, which I would support them through. Although many had good reason to be frustrated by the system, the truth of the matter was that they were grieving unbearable losses, and being angry about a procedural issue gave them back some control in an utterly powerless situation. When we're feeling threatened or powerless and, in turn, respond angrily, we can shut down our ability to see our path clearly. Although my clients may have well and truly been justified in their responses, the underlying cause of their anger was, in most cases, their grief, pain and loss.

Even in our everyday lives, we can find ourselves responding angrily to minor irritations, which can get in the way of moving forward. As a parent who has to direct the many lanes of traffic in a busy household, sometimes the most trivial things cause the biggest blow-ups. Children not listening, or bothering you when you have to complete an array of tasks in a time crunch. Stubbing your toe on the doorframe when you're scrambling to get ready. Children not getting dressed. Can't find the lunch box. Where are the keys!? Any one of these inconsequential moments can lead to an explosive outburst (often regretted instantaneously), which is really about the anxiety or stress we might be feeling, totally unrelated to the doorframe, or the shoes, or the lunch box.

When these moments happen infrequently or only during moments of stress and overwhelm, you could just consider it collateral damage in the war of life. It's when these instances begin to become the norm, the levels of anger increase and the outbursts become more unpredictable that you should start to consider what might be going on.

You might have already guessed by now that the whole premise of this book is to encourage you to open yourself up to the possibilities that lie ahead, so, if anger is holding you back, it's time to move through it.

Digging Deep

The first step is recognising the impact that it might have on your life. If you find yourself feeling angry or reactive to change in any aspect of your life, consider why this might be.

There may be patterns of behaviour that can be attributed to the feelings that underlie your anger. Pay attention if you find yourself responding to questions or situations in a way that feels out of character or if you're suddenly overreacting to things that wouldn't normally ruffle your feathers. Once you've had a moment to stop and reflect, try to unpack what is at the core of the issue. Peel back the layers and see the situation from a macro perspective and ask yourself, what else is happening in my life at the moment? Where are my stress points? What am I feeling anxious about? Have I responded this way before in a different setting? Digging down into the core of the unresolved issue is a good place to start, but the work doesn't end there.

Often, we think that once we've worked out what the links are, our work is done. Unfortunately, all we've done here is patch up the wound, but the feeling or feelings at the core of the issue lie ready and waiting to pounce at the next available opportunity.

So, do some reflecting. What is really going on? How far back does this issue go? Is it a result of childhood experiences? Things that have occurred in the workplace? In relationships?

With family? Consider whether there might be valid reasons for you to be lashing out or responding to situations in a negative way.

Try to take yourself out of the current situation that has caused you to react that way, and think about your life as a whole. If there are feelings that could be resolved through some work on some of the background noise, like anxiety, self-esteem, grief or fear, then perhaps that's where you need to start. Clearing the noise will allow you to make the space to embrace new opportunities.

Raging Against the Machine

We know that anger creates incredible energy, and not necessarily in a positive sense. It also takes a lot of energy to maintain and just isn't good for us. Consider whether there are ways you could channel that energy into something constructive for yourself. Let it out through exercise or throw it into something creative. Get your body moving and get yourself out of your head. Exercise in itself is a great way to release endorphins, which reduce stress and help to make you feel more positive, which then gives you the space to do that reflecting. While you're at it, spend some time in that space experimenting with mindfulness activities, meditation, yoga, breath work – things that help to ground you and bring you back into your body.

Navigating our way through life can be a tangled web of mashed-up connections and misfires that trip us up and slow us down. Try not to let the frustration seep in when that does inevitably happen. Take a moment, cool down, figure it out and let it go. Holding onto the rage or frustration only causes us more harm in the long run and prevents us from finding the path that will elevate us in a personal or professional way.

Box it out, run it out or walk it out, and give yourself permission to feel what needs to be felt, then build up that confidence to move through it.

Hack

Anger is often about something else.

Check in

What am I really feeling here?

Self-talk

There is probably more to this story; is there another way to look at this?

The Work

Practise calming strategies that work for you. Find an outlet for that energy. Reflect on what might be bubbling away under the surface of your anger and address those feelings. Do not beat yourself up for your reactions, and treat yourself with kindness.

Attitude

When you think about a big change taking place, like moving house or starting a new job, chances are you'll probably have an immediate, internal reaction. You might think, 'Amazing! I'm so ready for a new challenge!' Or you might think, 'That'd be right. Just when I'm feeling safe and secure, the next thing happens to make my life difficult again'. It's an ingrained, knee-jerk reaction that reveals the truth about the way we see ourselves and our lives, and sets the tone for the steps that follow.

Of course, there are thousands of other ways we might react to a change in our environment or in our lives, but how we perceive the opportunity and, in turn, respond to it can have everything to do with our attitude.

You have probably heard people being identified as having a good attitude, that they're seen as having a positive outlook on life. Or maybe you've heard people being called out for having a bad attitude somewhere along the line. Perhaps at school you heard a teacher refer to another student, or maybe even to you, as having a 'bad attitude' and this was given as the explanation for poor behaviour or poor choices. 'They're a great kid, but they've got a terrible attitude.'

It's often a throwaway line that's used to describe someone's character and the rationalisation for their not reaching their potential. Attitude can be used as a bit of a scapegoat in behaviour management and in social settings. Football coaches use it, teachers use it, even the women on *The Real Housewives* use it as a pop psychology assessment of a person's perceived failings.

Attitude isn't as simple as having a good one or a bad one, and there are always plenty of factors that contribute to it. These can be internal and external factors. Our level of stress, prior experiences, self-talk and expectations are all part of the equation.

When we're talking about embracing change, attitude does have a key part to play.

Self-fulfilling Prophecy

When I was studying psychology at university, I remember learning about the concept of a self-fulfilling prophecy. I was struck by the idea that other people's opinions of us can shape who we actually become, whether positively or negatively. A well-known study on self-fulfilling prophecy in an educational setting was conducted by Rosenthal and Jacobson[8] in 1968. They found that when teachers had positive or higher expectations of students, the students elevated their performance to meet the expectation. In fact, in many cases they performed even better than expected. This was known as the Pygmalion effect.

Conversely, when teachers had negative or lower expectations of students, those students responded negatively by meeting those lower expectations. Often this included lower performance scores and increased problematic behaviour. This was known as the Golem effect.

The experiment has been replicated over the years and each time the outcome has remained the same – behaviour can be influenced by outside expectations.

It's an interesting concept that we rise or fall to meet the expectations of the person who created them. It gives a lot more weight to the responsibility of parents and educators to consider the kind of influence and impact they might be having, even in a subliminal way, on the young people in their care.

Thinking back on your own childhood, was there ever a time when someone important told you that you couldn't do something well? For example, I often hear people say they're not creative. If we have been told that we're not creative by a teacher or by someone close to us like a parent or a person we respect, under the Golem effect, it is likely that we will believe it. As a result, we may not even attempt to explore our creativity and may close ourselves off from the possibilities.

I also often hear from clients that they're not good at sport. Again, if we've been treated differently to the star athletes in the group at school, we may believe we're not athletic or not good at sport. Perhaps we have found it difficult at times or can't quite keep up with the run times of the naturally gifted runners in the class. If the coach or the trainer didn't show us that they believed in us, why would we believe in ourselves? Sadly, this can mean that we give up before we've really even tried. And so it becomes a self-fulfilling prophecy, a vicious little cycle – limiting ourselves, preventing us from exploring and developing, and keeping our perspective narrow.

How awful that the expectations of others can have such a direct influence on our own beliefs about ourselves. Thankfully, we can overcome this. Every experience we have creates a happy little breeding ground for our attitude to develop, often without us even realising.

Reach for the Calculator

If you have read the Anxiety chapter in this book, you will recall the story I shared about refusing to go to school out of fear that my teacher was going to call me out or that I would embarrass myself for not knowing all of my times tables. I had seen my teacher react in a scary way to other students who had not performed the way she would have liked and, therefore,

We can become
whatever people
tell us we are.

felt scared myself. I didn't feel as though she paid the same level of attention to me during maths as she did to the small handful of children who excelled in numeracy. I began to believe that I wasn't good at maths at that tender age of 8 and, as a result, I developed a negative attitude towards it and gave up trying. It wasn't immediate, but gradual over the years. At first, I didn't like it, it made me anxious. Then I actually believed it was too hard and would zone out.

It wasn't that I had any real evidence that I wasn't good at maths, I just believed the narrative I had created in my head and from the encounters in my external world, which developed into a negative attitude towards numbers. So much so that I wouldn't really apply myself in the same way that I would in other areas of study or interests. To this day, I still find myself zoning out and avoiding numbers when the opportunity arises.

If we're ever out together for a meal and you see me staring blankly at the bill when it arrives, don't be fooled into thinking I'm working out how we split it. I'm just zoning out with my negative attitude to numbers and waiting for you to figure it out for us.

However, the good news is, attitude is not permanent. It can absolutely change.

Reframe Your Brain

The trick is to recognise when you're having these negative thoughts about yourself and to reframe them. It's not an overnight miracle cure, but by noticing the patterns of thinking that exist, we can begin to challenge them and change them.

In my case for example, when next confronted with a dinner bill that needs to be split three ways, instead of thinking, 'Oh God, there's no point even trying to work that out!', I could reframe it by saying, 'Easy! I'll just grab my calculator and figure it out'. So, I'm not trying to convince myself that I'm suddenly a division master and can split up a bill in the blink of an eye. But what I am doing is changing my attitude about being confronted with a mathematical equation and finding a solution that works for me. By finding another solution (the calculator) and resolving any fear or anxiety I might have felt about having to work it out in my head in front of other people, I have shown myself there is another way to look at it – and it doesn't have to be so scary.

When we reframe something, it's not about convincing ourselves of something unbelievable or unattainable. It's about trying to find another way to look at the situation, to change our negative attitude to something more positive. Doing this is imperative to open ourselves up to opportunities and to encourage ourselves to nudge our way out of our comfort zone.

Light and Shade

It's not just about thinking positively, in fact, that's something that is certainly not realistic 24/7. We're not always going to find the positive in everything – and that is okay! It's more important to find a healthy balance and accept that we're not going to love everything, we're not going to feel happy all the time and we're not necessarily going to be good at everything.

Sometimes we're sold the happiness agenda, which ascribes to the belief that we should be striving to be happy all the time. That is just not feasible, nor is it reality, and it can be more damaging than actually allowing ourselves to experience the inevitable highs and the lows of life.

Once we've accepted that there is going to be discomfort and there are going to be parts of our lives that we're not thrilled about, we can find ways to be comfortable in that space without fighting it. To put it simply, if we change our thinking, we can change our attitude. In my case, the calculator negates my number negativity.

The reason attitude is so important is because it directly relates to our thoughts about ourselves and our place in the world. As we know, our thoughts impact our emotions and how we feel about ourselves. If we *think* that we're not worthy of a new experience, a promotion or a healthy relationship, we will absolutely believe that. This might lead us into staying in situations that are not good for us or deprive us

By noticing
the patterns of
thinking that exist,
we can begin to
challenge them and
change them.

of the opportunity to grow and try new things. Resolving our attitude about change allows us to open the door to the possibilities in our lives. Instead of responding to our first reaction to the idea, take a moment to sit back and look at the bigger picture. Shake off any preconceived notions of what you could or should be doing and prepare to launch yourself right out of the little box you might have put yourself into. Change the narrative so that you're the first person championing your moves in the background. Then, create your own expectations about yourself and your life, and get ready to start living up to those instead.

Hack

Our attitudes are not fixed. They can change with a little shift in our perspective.

Check in

What is my immediate reaction to the idea of change?

Self-talk

It's okay not to love this; it doesn't mean I can't do it.

The Work

Practise reframing any negative thoughts that come up when you notice you're having an adverse reaction to something. Notice the opportunities to practise. Make a note of any automatic thoughts you might have about situations or events, then write out what you could say to reframe them. Notice when you're having a positive reaction or automatic thought and commend yourself for that. Consider a calculator solution to the things that make you uncomfortable. Practise being comfortable in discomfort.

Passion

For some people, the question is not '*how* do I take the leap and reach my dreams?' but actually, 'what *is* my dream?' That in itself can be a huge deterrent when it comes to opening up to the possibilities that life may have in store for you. Thinking that you lack passion means that you may in fact be missing the opportunities that are right in front of your eyes.

I remember a conversation a number of years ago with a friend who was genuinely enthusiastic and supportive of my most recent professional pivot at the time. She lamented that she just couldn't think of anything she was very passionate about and that she wished she was more adventurous in life. That conversation struck a chord in me as, until that point, I had not considered that anyone would be living a life without passion or without at least seeking out new experiences.

For my friend, however, she described her life as full of the mundane. A cycle of waking up, going to work, coming home and lying on the couch. Of course, there were holidays and nights with friends, she said, but she felt that she just didn't have any real hobbies or interests to pursue, and so she never really pushed herself outside of her very cosy little comfort zone.

The reason this stayed with me is that it made me feel a bit sad. I was sad that my friend appeared to be missing the zest in her life that could spark new interests and exploration. I was also sad that she had described her life as mundane, when it was really anything but that. It certainly wasn't that she was boring – in fact, I would describe her as the exact opposite. It was more a case of becoming accustomed to a routine that kept her busy, but not evolving.

This is not a condition that was unique to my friend. In fact, I think many of us would agree that there have been times in our lives when we have found ourselves languishing in a job that is no longer teaching us new things or in a relationship that we may have outgrown – where we have lost our drive and enthusiasm or have simply just come to the end of a chapter in life.

Passion is not something just reserved for the passionate. It's a way of encapsulating that innate human desire to seek out new ventures and pursue new experiences. We are all capable of finding our passion, but it won't look the same for everyone. We need to redefine the concept and take the pressure off ourselves. What piques my interest is not necessarily going to pique yours – and that's okay. It doesn't make me better than you if I have an idea of what I'd like to learn more about and you're not sure yet.

We are all
capable of finding
our passion, but it
won’t look the same
for everyone.

For some, being passionate about technology would be incredibly thrilling, but, for others, might be quite dull. A keen interest in film, language, music or physical activity won't excite us all equally. Finding new ways to spend time together as a family could be joyful for some and tedious for others. The way each idea lights us up is as unique as we are.

It's important to note, however, that passion doesn't need to have anything to do with career aspirations or hobbies at all; it can simply be infused into the way we approach life. The idea is not to try to drum up excitement about somebody else's interests, but to get really curious about your own.

Passion as a concept is a little bit misleading when it comes to taking that leap of faith. We are often told that in order to follow our dreams, and before we take the leap, we need to have that fire in the belly, that all-knowing sense that we are on the right track. That we must be entirely certain about something and have all our ducks in a row before we can take a chance and try it. That we need to trust our gut. While that may be true for some things, it's not very realistic and would leave so many of us wasting away in the dead ends, with no escape in sight. If we wait until we have it all figured out, we could be waiting a very long time.

Light the Spark

Passion and interest are about exploration. It's about finding something that ignites your curiosity and staying curious about the world around you.

If you find yourself reading this and thinking, 'I'm not a very passionate person. I'd love to try something new, but I don't even know where to begin!' then just start somewhere. Make a list of all the things that you have ever been interested in, even the tiniest bit. It might seem a silly or pointless exercise, but all you're trying to do is awaken that part of you that was once in awe of new things.

As children, we are in a constant state of wonder. Everything is exciting and new, thrilling and of interest. Just learning new words or discovering that people have ideas that we haven't had before is exhilarating. Try to fire up the child inside of you who is eager to breathe in new experiences and try things without fear. The key is to commit to the exploration and to let go of the notion that you need to commit to an entirely new path.

Have some fun! Take yourself to a wine and painting class. You may not become the next Rothko, but you might discover you'd like to know more about winemaking. You might even broaden your social circle by discovering like-minded people. Talk to others about what they do for fun, or what projects they might have started or even completed in lockdown.

Read articles from cities around the world, and discover art and music that we might not have been exposed to at home. Go down an Instagram rabbit hole looking for people who inspire you, even just the slightest bit.

Being passionate is not a skill that is exclusive to a particular type of person – we can all discover ways to be zealous about life and continue to learn and grow. Don't let a negative mindset prevent you from trying new things. Life is yours for the taking, to ravish and enjoy. It is not just reserved for 'others' to grab at. You are every bit as deserving of a life full of joy and wonder and, most certainly, a life filled with passion.

Hack

We can all ignite passion in our lives, just start small.

Check in

When was the last time I tried something new?

Self-talk

What can I get curious about today?

The Work

Make that list of things that spark your interest, even in the tiniest way: new foods, wines, hobbies, interests, languages, ways of moving your body, music, books, films you haven't seen before. Get messy, have a bath, try a skin scrub, style your hair differently. Try something new every day and reawaken the child within. Reawaken your childlike curiosity.

Gratitude

This chapter runs the risk of sounding a little bit 'woo-woo', but there is actual science behind the concept of gratitude and what it can do for our brains. Promise.

Gratitude is something that may not immediately spring to mind when wondering about making a change in your life – in a similar way that attitude may not. However, it's the nuances of thinking and mindset that make all the difference.

Gratitude, put simply, is the practice of being grateful for the things that come our way, for the people in our lives or for our position in life. It doesn't mean we adopt a Pollyanna-style approach to life and endlessly express the wonderful things about life, but it does mean making a conscious effort to pause and reflect and consider the things that might bring us joy – to name and acknowledge the things we are thankful for.

In doing this, we gradually replace any potentially negative outlook with a positive one, reminding ourselves to look for the good in our lives. In essence, it's about choosing to see the glass as half full.

With gratitude,
we gradually replace
any potentially
negative outlook
with a positive one,
reminding ourselves
to look for the good
in our lives.

You might be wondering what this has to do with decision-making or our flexibility in terms of making change. Gratitude is equally as important as attitude in that it shapes our view of the world and, in turn, directly impacts our adaptability and readiness to embrace new challenges as they arise.

Research into gratitude and its effect on wellbeing and outlook was first conducted by two psychologists, Emmons and McCullough,[9] in 2003. Their original study found that people who practise gratitude have greater levels of positive expression, more sleep, better sleep quality, greater optimism and a sense of connectedness to others. They also found that participants in their study who practised gratitude had higher levels of wellbeing. Other outcomes included a higher level of prosocial behaviour, meaning that participants were more likely to offer support to others. What a lovely side effect, that by changing our own perspective it is not only good for us but for those around us too.

The Power of Gratitude

Someone who has taken the practice of gratitude to the next level is business owner Claire Summers, whom I chatted with on the podcast. Claire discovered the power of gratitude through the afternoon ritual of watching *Oprah* from her couch at home. At the time when *Oprah* was on our screens at 3pm every day, the concept of gratitude was still fairly left of centre. Claire remembers hearing Oprah Winfrey talk about it and something resonating within her.

As a young woman, Claire found herself in an unhealthy relationship and then became pregnant. At the same time, she reconnected with her father after some time apart, who informed her that he was dying from terminal cancer. Tragically, it wasn't long after that news that Claire suffered a miscarriage. Through that, she came to the realisation that she needed to leave her relationship. After suffering pregnancy loss and the end of this relationship, Claire nursed her father through his final days.

Following those difficult days, and with plenty of time for reflection, Claire decided to take her fertility into her own hands and create an insurance policy for herself, for that hopeful day when the time came to try for a family again.

But the hits kept coming, with Claire almost losing her life to ovarian hyperstimulation syndrome during the process of freezing her eggs for the future. After eleven days in hospital, in and out of consciousness, and a long recovery at home with her mum, Claire became deeply depressed.

During that dark time, Claire made the decision to pull herself through the cumulative pain and sadness and to try to spark some light and positivity into her outlook. She began creating little gratitude cards to fill a glass jar.

Each morning and night, she would write one sweet note to herself to remind herself that it wasn't all as bad as it felt. Sometimes those notes were as simple as being grateful for the fact that she had slept that night, that she had eaten or that she was able to get out of bed that day. Bit by bit, she felt the fog begin to clear from her mind.

Claire would be forgiven entirely for believing that the hand she had been dealt was incredibly unfair and that perhaps the world was not as rosy as some would lead us to believe. Instead of crumbling in a heap, she actively made a choice to find the rose among the thorns and to reframe her thinking about herself and her situation. In doing this, Claire was able to transform her thoughts and feelings, which led her to make significant changes to her life and direction.

One of those changes was turning her glass jar of gratitude into a little side hustle that, through a twist of fate, saw Oprah Winfrey herself catapult the gratitude jars into an overnight global success, when she named them one of her famous Oprah's Favourite Things in 2017. From watching Oprah talk about gratitude from her couch in the afternoons, to being on stage with Oprah being awarded with accolades and recognition was the sweetest serendipity that Claire could have ever imagined.

We could all have our own Oprah moments waiting around the next corner. That's the beauty of life: you never know what's coming next. But, by actively opting to find the positive, no matter how small or trivial it may seem at the time, and by choosing the narrative that we play through our mind, we all have the ability to improve our wellbeing and become a better version of ourselves.

How do we actually practise the art of gratitude? It can be as simple as keeping a gratitude journal or, like Claire, writing a little note to yourself each day. Perhaps you might prefer to add a note to your paper or electronic diary at the beginning or the end of each day. The key is not to become complacent about it and just make generic statements about your life to yourself. The change in our thinking and in our brain comes from dynamic action, meaning we have to keep our brain on its toes. Just simply saying things like 'I'm grateful for my life' or 'I'm grateful for my family' doesn't train your brain to look for the moments to be thankful for and we can run the risk of tuning ourselves out. By drilling down to the detail, saying something like 'I'm grateful for the big hug my son gave me today', as opposed to just being grateful for family, means we have to actually do the work and, in turn, receive the benefits of change. Over time, our brains will rewire to automatically seek out the moments of gratitude, and we will reap the rewards from both a psychological and a wellbeing perspective.

What are you grateful for today?

Hack

Gratitude is not about pretending everything is great, it's about discovering what you are thankful for.

Check in

Can I focus on what I do have, rather than what I lack?

Self-talk

I am going to notice one new thing I'm grateful for today.

The Work

Make a ritual out of your gratitude practice. Choose a medium to express yourself in, whether electronic or handwritten, and schedule it into your day each day. See if you can notice things that you might be thankful for throughout the day too, expanding your practice across your life. Try to think of moments that captured you before leaving the house in the morning, something that happened at work, an interaction with a friend or loved one, something you read or watched that you connected with. Each moment is valid and worthy of noting, as long as it resonated with you for a moment. The more you practise doing this, the more habitual it will become and, in turn, the greater impact it will have on your wellbeing. Think about paying it forward. Can you tell someone why you're grateful for them today?

Joy

We've tackled some pretty heavy content throughout the pages of this book, as we have flexed our cognitive muscles through some of the biggest barriers to change. While we have been reflecting over the things that hold us back and prevent us from taking a chance in life, it's important to remember that, in all of the work we do on ourselves and in our lives, it's imperative that we find joy.

Our hearts and our minds are constantly evolving, and we will always have work we could be doing to improve our understanding of how and why we behave and respond to the stressors of life. Our emotions will always be like an ocean of waves, filled with highs and lows, rising and crashing to the shore. Sometimes life will feel like a breezy summer holiday and other times we'll be thrashed around and find ourselves thumping against the sandbar. We just have to learn to roll with the tide.

Imagine yourself being caught in a rip. Hopefully you know that if you struggle against it, you can quickly exhaust your energy reserves and risk drowning, while still getting no closer to the shore. In that situation, the advice from lifeguards is to stay calm, float with the current or swim parallel to the shoreline until you pop up out of the grip of the current and can swim safely to shore. Giving in to the power of the ocean can be incredibly frightening, and rolling with the tide can feel counterintuitive at the time, but the alternative is far more dangerous.

Managing the depths of our feelings is much the same. If we fight against them, ignore the warning signs and burn ourselves out, we are rendering ourselves helpless against the tide. We need to take our time, find the moments of calm, roll onto our backs and float. Trust that the tide will carry us through. Take a moment to appreciate the beauty of the sun rippling across the water and admire the strength of the sea.

To be quite honest, I'm not sure how much joy I could find mid-panic in the churning of a rip-tide, but, in an emotional sense, there is always a way to reach for the glimmer of joy.

Last night, it was one of those evenings. I had one child who was unwell and had to stay home from child care, another who was overtired from a big day at kinder, topped off by an unavoidably busy day for both my partner and I. Having a sick child at home threw a massive wrench into our plans. We adapted to the modified plan, changed the order of our day, divided up the tasks relating to our little sick child and managed to get as much done as we could. Our little one had been asking for gnocchi all day from his makeshift bed on the couch and, taking this as a good sign that he was starting to feel better, I dashed out to the shops to buy the ingredients. Instead of the dinner we had planned, I cooked up delicious, healthy, veggie-packed gnocchi. When we finally all sat down to the table, little Mr Sick decided he 'hated' gnocchi and refused to sit with us at the table. Instead, he threw himself back on the couch, tried to hide, played with his toys and did everything he could to gain our attention from his corner of the room. Meanwhile our kindergarten kid was eating all the gnocchi but not the vegetables (cooked to perfection, I might add) and I was trying to manage him and the little one from the other corner of the room, while becoming increasingly frustrated with them both. It was a battle of wills that included every kind of strategy, threat and trick in the book until finally, almost an hour later, the little one was being spoonfed and chewing like a snail, the older one was moving the veggies around in the bowl, both were loud and obnoxious, and I was ready to lose it.

Feeling the dark cloud of rage gathering above my head and the scowl getting more deeply ingrained in my face, in an effort to distract us all, I put on a song that my eldest had been singing at kinder that day. We started to sing together in an attempt to tune out the frustration. Suddenly I had a silly idea and leapt up from the table, all six eyes following me and wondering what I was up to. I returned moments later in a wide-brimmed red felt hat and a big, fluffy faux-fur coat hastily thrown on over my apron and started dancing around to the music like I was a teenager at a music festival.

The boys giggled and my eldest picked up the vibe. He disappeared down the hallway and came back in a white, woollen beanie of mine and started dancing alongside me. We cracked up laughing and watched his face light up with pride. Thrilled with his reception, he ran back to the bedroom and came out again in his dad's straw fedora and a pair of my activewear leggings encasing his little frame all the way up to his armpits and looking more like a full bodysuit. He started dancing like a mini Channing Tatum/Usher mashup, wiggling and krumping like there was no tomorrow. Needless to say, he had us all roaring with laughter, the tears streaming down our cheeks. The whole family got in on the action, dressing up in funny hats and outfits and having a boogie to some of our favourite songs, laughing and giggling at each other's silliness.

Through the ultimate frustration and absolute exasperation after a difficult day and the utterly infuriating dinner, we had all managed to find joy. The joy was infectious. That joy carried us through the bath and bedtime routine with ease, with nothing but love and elation emanating from our hearts.

It could absolutely have gone the other way had I allowed my temper and fatigue to get the better of me. There's no doubt that we could have all gone to bed that night feeling frustrated and, in my children's case, probably a little emotionally bruised by my inability to find the lightness and let go of the dark when things weren't going smoothly. We would all have suffered if I had fought against the tide instead of rolling onto my back and floating for a while.

It's not always going to feel that accessible to be able to turn our frustration into moments of joy, but it's a practice that takes time and patience, and a willingness to try.

There's a well-known saying that goes something like, 'you can't taste the sweet without the sour', and it's the truth. We also can't wait for the ever-changing landscape of our mental health to improve in order to experience joy or to believe that joy is the endgame we're working towards. Why deprive ourselves of the moments in the sun between the bouts of rain?

We need to take the time to ensure we're infusing joy into all aspects of our lives – not in a maniacally happy, masking-all-the-other-feelings kind of joy, but true and honest joy in the moments that we need it. If we are waiting to get through the hard parts before we give ourselves permission to enjoy the journey, the work we are doing becomes meaningless and more challenging as we grind away.

For some, it might come from time with family, or time alone. It might be through the nourishment of seeing friends or from doing something you love. If you're a Marie Kondo convert, perhaps it comes from minimal possessions kept neatly in a well-organised wardrobe. Maybe, like me, it's just about finding a crack in the mood and tearing it open with some silliness and laughter.

The important thing is to ensure that there are moments of joy throughout the course of the day that help to keep us balanced and stop us from tumbling down a dark path of deep introspection and a focus on the negative. It's about creating emotional resilience through active participation in *all* of

It's about creating emotional resilience through *all* of the thoughts and feelings, and challenging ourselves to find the light.

the thoughts and feelings that encompass our minds, and challenging ourselves to find the light throughout.

In other words, we have to do the work and engage in the practice of finding the joy in order to benefit from it. We can't expect it to just happen, or, worse, that it will only happen when all the work is over. Don't wait for the journey to be over to allow yourself to smile.

From the Inside Out

We know that the expressions of joy and happiness cause dopamine and serotonin (the neurotransmitters or chemicals that make us feel good) to be released in our brain, having a flow-on effect to our nervous systems and our bodies. Amazingly, we can actually trick our brains into releasing these chemicals simply by smiling.

If you've been doing the hard yards through the chapters of this book, working on anxiety or self-esteem or anything else at all, take a moment to remind yourself to smile. Sometimes it's as simple as that. Start with a smile, release those neurotransmitters and bask in the physical response. Do that once, do it again and keep going until smiling and finding the moments of joy become habitual through the inevitable ebbs and flows of life.

Use the smile as a circuit-breaker for stress and choose to step out of the mire. When we do that, we begin to see more of the lightness and become practised at active mindfulness – being in the moment and pulling ourselves into the positive.

Embrace That Change

I hope that, through the pages of this book, the notion of change has become a much less daunting prospect. I challenge you to look for the hidden opportunities that may be glimmering in the sand, no longer easily overlooked. Step out of your comfort zone and take a risk – no matter how small – knowing that it may well become your greatest reward.

Embracing change is about embracing all of the parts of ourselves: the good, the bad and the ugly. When we accept them and work through them, we'll find those shimmering moments of joy.

Good luck, and go get them!

Hack

Give yourself permission to take a moment to find the light.

Check in

When was the last time I smiled? How can I let go of the negative feelings associated with my task and let some sunlight in?

Self-talk

I'm going to fake it till I make it, baby!

The Work

You can absolutely fake your way into a happiness response with a simple smile. Start there and then work outwards. If you're feeling the frustration building, where can you instil a moment of joy to break up the tension? Let go of what came before or what's coming up next, take a deep breath in through the nose and, as you slowly let it go, find a little chink in the armour and push yourself to notice or do something that will delight you in the smallest of ways.

Caveat

This book comes with a huge caveat and the implicit understanding that there are many reasons why the information in these pages may not be appropriate for you.

For anyone who is suffering from significant mental health disorders or has suffered trauma in their lives, I would always recommend seeking professional help to work through the more complex issues first. This book can be the icing on the cake once you have addressed the underlying concerns. There is absolutely no shame in needing to access professional help; in fact I thoroughly recommend it for everyone – therapists included!

If you're wondering where to start, head to your GP and talk to them about a referral to a psychiatrist or to enquire about a Mental Health Treatment Plan that will provide you with up to twenty subsidised sessions with a psychologist or registered social worker.

Most psychologists use CBT (cognitive behaviour therapy) and this is what the Australian Government has identified as meeting the criteria for rebates. However, there are many incredible therapists who work beyond the scope of the CBT framework who may not be eligible for Medicare rebates. Don't be put off by that! Therapy is not a one-size-fits-all modality, nor should it ever be.

I would suggest doing some research into the various therapeutic frameworks that exist around your issue of concern and then asking for recommendations for a therapist who might work in that field. Some of the most transformative work occurs outside the government's narrow view of what meets rebated therapy ideals.

Some of the therapeutic frameworks that resonate with me and that have been successful for many of my clients (through other practitioners) are:

- eye movement desensitisation and reprocessing (EMDR)
- art therapy
- positive psychology
- internal family systems
- family therapy
- hypnotherapy
- emotion-focused therapy (EFT)
- attachment-based therapy

- sex therapy
- narrative therapy
- mindfulness-based cognitive therapy
- family constellations

Therapy is like any relationship in our lives; you're not always going to click with everyone or make a lasting connection with every therapist you meet. It is absolutely okay to try someone on for size, work out if there's a good connection and find out whether you feel comfortable with their therapeutic and interpersonal style. You will know if they're the right fit for you by how comfortable you feel sharing your story and digging into some of the layers with them. Any good therapist will not be offended if it's not the right fit for you.

Therapy can feel like a scary process, and the idea of having to sit down in front of a complete stranger and reveal the most vulnerable parts of your life might be so overwhelming that it stops you before you even start. It's important to remember that you are in control. The time you have together is there for you to share as much or as little as you feel able to each time. If it's moving too fast, you can slow it right down. If the focus doesn't feel right, change it. Even if it's not always the easiest path, therapy is a change well worth embracing.

Some useful links to keep in your back pocket:

- www.lifeline.org.au (crisis support and suicide prevention)
- www.suicidecallbackservice.org.au (suicide prevention)
- www.thehotline.org (domestic violence support)
- www.beyondblue.org.au (mental health support)
- www.blueknot.org.au (complex trauma support)
- https://butterfly.org.au (support for eating disorders and body image)
- https://mensline.org.au (counselling service for men)
- www.relationships.org.au (relationship support for individuals, couples and families)
- https://parentline.com.au (support for parents and carers)
- www.goodtherapy.com.au/find_a_therapist.php (find an accredited psychotherapist, counsellor, family therapist, social worker or psychologist)

Acknowledgements

This book was an absolute leap of faith for me. However, the road to embracing my own change began a few steps before this, with the conviction and belief of my manager Dean Buchanan. Dean was the first person to encourage me to stop burying my credentials and acknowledge my breadth of experience. Without Dean recognising this little diamond hiding very much in the rough, this book would not exist. Thank you, Dean, for your hours (and hours) of support and encouragement, and for challenging me to move through my own insecurities and be honest with myself about the next incarnation of my life. Without you and without your support, this opportunity would never have even arisen. I am so very grateful to have you in my corner.

To Martin Hughes and Keiran Rogers of Affirm Press, thank you for presenting me with this incredible opportunity to grow and evolve, and to spread my wings in a new way. Thank you for patiently working through my own bouts of imposter syndrome and assuring me that I was on the right track, every time I was second-guessing myself. Having your unwavering support and the backing of such accomplished professionals has been a repeated 'pinch me' experience. Thank you for believing in me, right from the start.

To my publisher Kelly Doust, your passion and enthusiasm have been an injection of pure joy. It has been a true honour to work with such a powerhouse of the publishing industry, and I can't quite believe that this work will sit alongside some of the most incredible books and talented people that I have long admired, as another feather to your cap. It has been an incredible blessing – thank you.

A special mention and huge thank you to Dianne Anderson, for holding the fort, managing the chaos and, in your usual unruffled style, taking it all in your stride while I squirrelled furiously away. Your support over the years has been unwavering, no matter what hurdle I continue to throw at you. I couldn't do our job without you, and I am so grateful for your encouragement as I try new things and add to the family, again and again. I hope you know how much I appreciate you.

To Kevin O'Brien, Harriet Empey and Armelle Davies – thank you for making the editing and copyediting process as seamless as you have. I was bracing myself for a journey, but it could not have been smoother or more enjoyable. I am grateful to each of you for your contributions and for your kind words and support.

Alissa Dinallo, thank you for your beautiful cover design. I fell in love at first glance! And to Emily Thiang, for your wonderful internal design to match.

To Layne Beachley, Sam Wood, Samantha Wills, Sarah Davidson, Olivia Rogers, Jules Sebastian, Michala Banas, Blair James and Claire Summers – thank you for going deep with me and for not being afraid to be vulnerable. I am filled with gratitude for each of you and will always treasure our time together. Thank you for allowing me to share parts of your stories again here.

Finally, a big thank you to my family for allowing me to unpack some of our real-life experiences within the pages of this book – from the day to day to the big stuff. A special thank you to Chris, for giving me the space to write, for wrangling the boys when I needed more time and for heroically weathering the storm when my anxiety would rise and come peppering down at the end of a busy day. Thank you for your consistent evenness, tempering my emotion. I love you and am so grateful to you.

References

1 Kübler-Ross, Elisabeth, 1969, *On Death and Dying*, Routledge, London.

2 Clance, Pauline Rose and Imes, Suzanne, 1978, 'The Imposter Phenomenon in High Achieving Women: Dynamics and Therapeutic Intervention', *Psychotherapy Theory, Research and Practice*, Vol. 15, No. 3, www.paulineroseclance.com/pdf/ip_high_achieving_women.pdf.

3 Beattie, Karen, '4 destructive traits of perfectionism, from Dr. Brené Brown', *The Growth Faculty*, 7 January 2019, www.thegrowthfaculty.com/blog/4destructivetraitsofperfectionismfromDrBrenBrown.

4 Goleman, Daniel, 1995, *Emotional Intelligence: Why It Can Matter More Than IQ*, Bantam Books, New York.

5 Freud, Sigmund, 1923, *Das Ich und das Es* (*The Ego and the Id*), Internationaler Psychoanalytischer Verlag, Vienna.

6 Erikson, Erik, 1950, *Childhood and Society*, W W Norton & Co., New York.

7 Piaget, Jean, 1923, *Le langage et la pensée chez l'enfant* (*The Language and Thought of the Child*), Delachaux et Niestlé, Neufchâtel and Paris.

8 Rosenthal, Robert and Jacobson, Lenore, 1968, *Pygmalion in the classroom: Teacher expectation and pupils' intellectual development*, Holt, Rinehart & Winston, New York.

9 Emmons, Robert and McCullough, Michael, 2003, 'Counting blessings versus burdens: an experimental investigation of gratitude and subjective well-being in daily life', *Journal of Personality and Social Psychology*, Vol. 84, No. 2, pp. 377–89.